Octoechos: Or The Book Of Eight Tones, A Primer Containing The Sunday Service In Eight Tones... - Primary Source Edition

Orthodox Eastern Church

OCTOECHOS

OR

THE BOOK OF EIGHT TONES

A PRIMER

CONTAINING

THE SUNDAY SERVICE IN EIGHT TONES

TRANSLATED

FROM THE SLAVONIAN FIRST EDITION OF 1891
PRINTED AT ST PETERSBURG AND PUBLISHED BY
THE MOST HOLY GOVERNING SYNOD OF RUSSIA

LONDON
J. DAVY & SONS
DRYDEN PRESS 137 LONG ACRE
1898

When He (the Highest) distributed the tongues of fire,
He called all to unity.

[*From the Contakion for the Holy Pentecost.*]

TO

HIS EMINENCE

THE RIGHT REVEREND NICHOLAS

LORD BISHOP OF ALEUT AND ALASKA,

WHOSE FATHERLY SOLICITUDE FOR THE SPIRITUAL WELFARE
OF THE YOUTH OF HIS UNIQUELY EXTENDED DIOCESE
HAS SUGGESTED THE TRANSLATION,

IS

THIS SECOND BOOK,

IN A BOLD, BUT HEARTFELT AND PRAYERFUL TRUST OF FURTHERING,
UNDER GOD, A GOOD CAUSE,

Most gratefully and humbly Dedicated,

BY

PROFESSOR N. ORLOFF,

THE TRANSLATOR,

The day of the Holy Trinity
(Whit-Sunday or Pentecost),
24th May / 5th June 1898.

KING'S COLLEGE,
LONDON, W.C.

ON SATURDAY

AT

The Great Vespers.

After the proemial Psalm, the usual portion of the Book of Psalms. For "O Lord, I have cried" there are appointed 10 *Stichoi, and we sing from the Octoechos* 3 *Sticheras of the Resurrection and* 4 *of the Eastern (Anatolian) and from the Minaion* 3 *or* 6.

The Sticheras of the Resurrection from the Octoechos, Tone 1.

ACCEPT our vespertine prayers, O Holy Lord, and grant us the remission of sins, for Thou alone hast made manifest unto the world the resurrection.

Go around Zion, O ye people, and encompass her * and give glory to Him Who in her midst arose from the dead, for He is our God that hath delivered us from our transgressions.

O come, ye people, let us hymn and bow down before Christ glorifying His resurrection from the dead, for He is our God that hath freed the world from the wiles of the enemy.

Other, Eastern (Anatolian) Sticheras, Tone 1.

Rejoice, O ye heavens †, sound the trumpets, ye foundations of the earth, thunder forth gladness, O ye mountains, for, behold, Emmanuel hath nailed to the cross our sins and the Giver of life hath slain death raising up Adam, as Lover of man.

Him Who in the flesh, for our sake and of His free will, was crucified, hath suffered, was buried and rose again from the dead, let us hymn, saying: Stablish in orthodoxy Thy Church, O Christ, and make our life peaceful, since Thou art good and Lover of man.

Before Thy life-bearing grave standing, we, unworthy, offer doxology to Thine ineffable tenderness of heart, O Christ our

---

* Psalm 47, 13. † Psalm 95, 11.

God, for the cross and the death hast Thou, O sinless One, accepted that Thou mightest grant resurrection unto the world, as Lover of man.

The Word, co-unoriginate and co-eternal with the Father, Who ineffably came forth from the virginal womb, Who of His free will and for our sake did accept both the cross and the death and rose up in glory, let us hymn, saying : O Lord, the Life-giver, glory to Thee, the Saviour of our souls.

Both now...the Theotokion :

Let us hymn Mary the Virgin that sprouted forth from the race of man and bore the Master of all,—her that is the glory of all the world,—the gate of the heaven, the chant of the bodiless and of the faithful the adornment; for she hath appeared both the heaven and the temple of the Godhead, she it was who having destroyed the partition-wall of enmity, brought in peace and opened the kingdom; therefore possessing in her the assurance of the faith, we have the defender in the Lord born of her. Take courage then, take courage, O ye God's people, for He shall vanquish the enemies, since He is all-powerful.

For Versicles the Sticheras of the Resurrection, Tone 1.

By Thy passion, O Christ, we have been set free from sufferings and by Thy resurrection have been delivered from corruption; O Lord, glory to Thee.

Other Sticheras in alphabetical† *order :*

Let the creation rejoice, let the heavens cheer, let the nations clap their hands for joy, for Christ our Saviour to the cross hath nailed our sins and having slain the death and raised up Adam —the progenitor of mankind, hath granted us life, as Lover of man.

Being the King of heaven and earth, Thou, incomprehensible, wast of Thy free will crucified through the love of man; Thee having met below, the hades was vexed*, whilst the souls of the righteous on receiving Thee were gladdened, and Adam seeing

---

* Isaiah 14, 9. † In the original Greek.

Thee—the Creator—in the nethermost parts, rose again. O wonder! How the life of all hath tasted death? but Thou desiredst to enlighten the world that crieth saying: Thou, risen from the dead, O Lord, glory to Thee.

The myrrh-bearing women, carrying spices, with haste and moaning reached Thy sepulchre, but not finding Thine all-purest body and from the angel having heard of the new and most glorious miracle, said to the Apostles: Risen is the Lord that granteth unto the world great mercy.

Glory...Both now...the Theotokion.

Behold, fulfilled is the prophecy of Isaiah*, for as Virgin hast thou borne and hast remained after giving birth just as before the birth, since the offspring was God, wherefore nature also was restored. Howbeit, O Mother of God, the supplications of thy servants that are being sent up to thee in thy temple, do not despise, but since thou hast borne in thine arms the merciful one, rather take compassion on thy servants and intercede that our souls may be saved.

The Troparion of the Resurrection, Tone 1.

Whilst the stone was sealed by the Jews, and at the time when the soldiers were guarding Thy most pure body, Thou didst arise on the third day, O Saviour, granting life to the world. Therefore the powers of the heavens cried out unto Thee, O Life-giver: Glory to Thy resurrection, O Christ, glory to Thy Kingdom, glory to Thine economy, O only Lover of man.

The Theotokion.

Whilst Gabriel was uttering to Thee, O Virgin: Hail! † with that voice was the Lord of all becoming incarnate in thee, the holy ark, ‡ as spake the righteous David; thou didst become wider than the heavens, whilst bearing thy Creator. Glory to Him that hath dwelt in thee; glory to Him that came forth from thee; glory to Him that hath delivered us through thy bringing forth.

---

* Isaiah 7, 14. † St. Luke 1, 28. ‡ Psalm 131, 8.

At Matins, after the 1*st Stichologia* (*portion of the Psalms*) *the Cathismata of the Resurrection, Tone* 1.

Whilst Thy sepulchre, O Saviour, was being guarded by soldiers, they became as dead from the brilliancy of the appearance of the angel that announced the resurrection unto the women. We glorify Thee, the Extirpator of corruption, we fall down before Thee that didst arise from the grave and art alone our God.

To the cross having been nailed of Thy free will, O Compassionate one, into the grave having been laid as dead, O Life-giver, Thou, O Mighty One, didst crush the dominating power by Thy death; for before Thee have trembled the gatekeepers of the hades, Thou hast raised together with Thyself those that died ages before, as the sole Lover of man.

Glory...Both now...the Theotokion.

Mother of God, that after the birth also appeared a veritable Virgin, art Thou known to us all who lovingly have recourse to thy goodness; for in thee we, sinners, possess intercession, thee we have acquired as salvation in temptations, O only all-blameless.

After the 2*nd Stichologia* (*portion of the Psalms*), *the Cathismata, Tone* 1.

Similar to Whilst the stone was sealed:

The women coming very early to the sepulchre and seeing the angel's apparition trembled: the grave being resplendent with life, the miracle struck them with amazement; therefore coming back they announced to the disciples the awaking. As the only mighty and strong, Christ hath captured the hades and raised together with Himself all those that perished, having through the power of the cross done away with the fear of condemnation.

To the cross wast Thou nailed, O Life of all, and among the dead wast Thou numbered*, O Lord immortal; Thou hast arisen on the third day, O Saviour, and raised Adam from

---

* Psalm 87, 5.

corruption. Therefore the powers of the heavens cried out unto Thee, O Christ the Life-giver: glory to Thy resurrection, glory to Thy condescension, O only Lover of man.

Glory...Both now...the Theotokion.

O Mary—the august receptacle of the Master—do raise up us that are fallen into the abyss of terrible despair, and of stumblings and afflictions; for thou art unto sinners, salvation and help and powerful intercession, and dost save thy servants.

Thereupon, the little Ectene and Hypakoe, Tone 1.

The repentance of the malefactor hath laid hold of the paradise, and the lamentation of the myrrh-bearing women joy hath announced, for risen art Thou, O Christ the God, granting to the world great mercy.

The Graduals: Antiphon 1*st, Tone* 1, *the verses being repeated:*

When I am in distress, do attend to my sorrows, O Lord, I cry unto Thee *.

The hermits continually long after God, they are outside the vain world.

Glory: Unto the Holy Ghost behoveth both honour and glory, just as unto the Father, together with the Son; let us therefore sing unto the Trinity as to a monarchy.

Both now...the same. Antiphon 2.

Unto the summits † of Thy laws hast Thou exalted me, make me sparkle with virtues, O God, that I may hymn Thee.

Taking me up with Thy right hand, do Thou, O Word, keep ‡ and preserve me lest the fire of sin scorch me.

Glory...

Of the Holy Ghost becometh renewed, every creature returning again to the primeval state, for He is co-equal in might with the Father and the Word.

---

* Psalm 119, 1. † Psalm 120, 1. ‡ Psalm 120, 5-7.

Both now...the same. Antiphon 3.

On account of those that said unto me: let us enter the courts of the Lord*, my spirit was gladdened, my heart rejoiceth.

In the house of David prevaileth great fear, for thrones being set therein†, all the tribes and nations of the earth shall be judged. *Glory...*

Unto the Holy Ghost it behoveth to offer honour, adoration, glory and power just as these appertain to the Father and to the Son, for the Trinity is one in substance, but not in persons.

Both now...the same. Prokeimenon, Tone 1.

Now will I arise, saith the Lord, I will set myself unto salvation, will not hesitate about it.

Verse: The words of the Lord are pure words (*Psalm* 11, 6, 7).

Every breath . . . . *The matutinal Gospel of the series.*

Having beheld the resurrection of Christ, let us adore the Holy Lord Jesus, the only sinless. Thy cross, O Christ, do we adore and Thy holy resurrection hymn and glorify; for Thou art our God, beside Thee we know none other, Thy name do we name. Come, all ye faithful, let us adore Christ's holy resurrection; for, behold, there is come through the cross joy unto all the world; ever blessing the Lord, we hymn His resurrection, for having endured crucifixion, by death He hath destroyed death.

Psalm 50: Have mercy on me, O God. *Glory...*

At the intercessions of the Apostles, O Merciful One, blot out the multitude of our sins. *Both now...*

At the intercessions of the Theotokos, O Merciful One, blot out the multitude of our sins. *Thereupon, Tone* 6:

Have mercy on me, O God, according to Thy great mercy; and according to the multitude of Thy compassions blot out my transgression ‡.

Thereupon this Stichera:

Having risen from the grave, as He foretold, Jesus hath granted us life eternal and great mercy.

---

* Psalm 121, 1. † Psalm 121, 5. ‡ Psalm 50, 3.

Save Thy people, O God...*And the exclamation:* By the mercy and compassions and love toward man...[*The Canon of the resurrection, Tone* 1].

Ode 1. *The Heirmos:*

Thy victorious right hand was God-beseemingly glorified in strength; for, O Immortal One, it hath, as all powerful, crushed the enemies and made for the Israelites the way along the depths of the sea.

The refrain: Glory, O Lord, to Thy holy resurrection. [*The Troparion:*]

Thou that with spotless hands from the earth, as God, hast in the beginning fashioned me, didst Thy hands spread on the cross, recalling from the earth my corruptible body which from the Virgin hast Thou taken.

Deprivation of life for my sake hast Thou suffered and Thy soul didst unto death deliver. Thou that hast with God's breath implanted in me the soul, having loosed it from eternal bonds and raised together with Thyself, Thou hast glorified it with incorruptibility. [*The Theotokion:*]

Hail Thou—the source of the grace; hail—the ladder and the gate of heaven; hail—both the candlestick and the golden pot and the uncut mountain—Thou that baredst unto the world Christ the Life-giver.

Another Canon of the cross and resurrection.

Ode 1. *The same Tone. Similar to:* Christ is being brought forth.

Christ deifieth me in His incarnation, Christ exalteth me through His humility, Christ delivereth me from suffering whilst He, the Life-giver, undergoeth the passion in His natural body; wherefore I sing the thanksgiving hymn: for He is glorified.

Christ exalteth me by His crucifixion, Christ raiseth me with Him by His being put to death, Christ granteth me life; wherefore clapping my hands for joy I sing to the Saviour the hymn of victory: for He is glorified. [*The Theotokion:*]

God, O Virgin, didst thou conceive and in thy virginity hast thou brought forth Christ that was incarnate of thee, O purest, —one Son that is hypostatically the Only-begotten and is known in two substances: for He is glorified.

Another Canon to the All-holy Theotokos. Ode 1. *The same Tone.*
Similar to: Thy victorious...

What hymn worthy of thee shall our inability offer unto thee? only the joyous one which Gabriel hath secretly taught us: Hail, O Theotokos-virgin, Mother unmarried.

Unto the Ever-virgin and Mother of the King of the highest powers, from the purest heart let us, O faithful, spiritually cry out: Hail, O Theotokos-virgin, Mother unmarried.

Immeasurable is the abyss of thine incomprehensible bringing forth, O purest; in faith then that admits of no doubt do we bring unto thee these words: Hail, O Theotokos-virgin, Mother unmarried. *Thereupon out of the Minaeon.*

Catabasis: I shall open my mouth...

Ode 3. *The Heirmos.*

O Thou that alone knowest the impotence of man's nature and hast compassionately taken it unto Thyself, do gird me with the power from on high, that I may cry out unto Thee: Holy is the living temple of Thine ineffable glory, O Lover of man.

Being God unto me, O Good One, Thou hast taken compassion of the fallen one, and having deigned to come down unto me, Thou hast exalted me by Thy crucifixion, so that I may cry out unto Thee: Holy is the living temple of Thine ineffable glory, O Lover of man.

Being life hypostatical, Thou, O Christ, hast as God compassionate put me on while in the state of corruption; having come down unto the mortal earth, Thou hast, O Master, destroyed the power of death, and having died and risen on the third day hast clothed me with immortality. [*The Theotokion:*]

Having conceived God in thy womb, O Virgin, by the All-holy Spirit, thou remainedst unconsumed, since the bush did clearly prefigure unto Moses the law-giver, thee being burnt, yet not scorched, that hast received the fire * unendurable.

---

* Isaiah 3, 2.

Another, The Heirmos : Before ages from the Father...

Unto Him Who on His shoulder the straying sheep had taken * and through the tree put down his sin, to Christ the God let us cry up: Thou that hast exalted our horn, art holy, O Lord.

To Him that did from the hades lead up the Great Shepherd Christ † and under His hierarchy by His apostles the nations manifestly tended—let us, O faithful, truthfully serve to the Divine Spirit.

Unto Him that of His will was without seed of the Virgin incarnate, unto the Son that hath His parent after the birth as pure Virgin by divine power preserved, unto Him that is God of all—let us cry up: Holy art Thou, O Lord.

Another, The Heirmos : O Thou that alone knowest.

A light cloud do we rightfully call thee, O Virgin, following the prophetic sayings, for sitting upon thee the Lord hath come to overthrow the seductions of Egypt—‡ the works of men's hands, and to enlighten those that serve them.

Thee the choir of prophets hath truly called a sealed spring and a door locked up §, clearly conveying to us the symbols of thine, O all-hymned, virginity, which thou didst preserve after the bringing forth also.

Having been vouchsafed to penetrate, as far as it was possible for him, the supersubstantial mind, Gabriel did bring unto thee, O all-spotless Virgin, a joyful message which clearly announced the conception of the Word and proclaimed thine ineffable bringing forth.

Ode 4. The Heirmos :

Thee as a mount overshadowed of God's grace having perceived with his prophetic eyes, Habbakuk hath proclaimed that out of thee shall issue forth the Holy One of Israel, for our salvation and restoration.

Who is this Saviour that cometh from Edom, wearing a crown

---

* Luke 15, 5. † Hebr. 13, 20. ‡ Isaiah 19, 1. § Song of Songs 4, 12.

of thorns, dressed in a red garment*, hanging upon a tree? He is the Holy One of Israel, for our salvation and restoration.

Behold, O ye mutinous people, and be ashamed, for He Whom ye out of madness begged Pilate to hang up on a cross, having destroyed the power of death is God-beseemingly risen from the grave. [*The Theotokion*:]

A tree of life we know thee, O Virgin; for it was not the deadly fruit that hath sprouted forth from thee for our consumption, but the delight of the life eternal, unto the salvation of us that are now hymning thee.

Another, The Heirmos: The staff out of the root of Jesse...

Who is this beautiful one from Edom, His garments dyed with the grapes of Bozrah? Beautiful He is because He is God and as man He is wearing a garment dyed red with the blood of flesh †. To Him we the faithful melodiously sing: Glory to Thy might, O Lord.

Christ having appeared a high priest of good things to come, hath destroyed our sin, and having shewn a novel way in His own blood, He hath entered into a better and more perfect tabernacle ‡, into the holy place, as our precursor.

[*The Theotokion*:]

Eve's ancient bond hast thou, O all-hymned, obtained by entreaty of the new Adam that is come for our sake; for having in unsullied conception united unto Himself intellectual, living flesh, from thee came forth Christ—one Lord in both natures.

Another, The Heirmos: Thee as a mount overshadowed...

Hear wonders, O heaven, and thou earth, give ear, for a daughter of the earthly and fallen Adam hath become Mother of God and her Maker, unto our salvation and restoration.

We sing thy great and terrible mystery, for having concealed it from the super-mundane orders, the Existing One hath descended upon thee, O all-hymned, as dew on wool, unto the salvation of us that hymn thee.

---

* Isaiah 63, 1, 2. † Isaiah 63, 1, 2. ‡ Hebr. 9, 11.

O holy of holies, all-hymned Theotokos, the longing of the peoples and the salvation of the faithful, from thee hath shone forth the Redeemer, Life-giver and Lord; Him importune that thy servants may be saved.

Ode 5. *The Heirmos:*

Thou that hast enlightened with the brightness of Thy coming, O Christ, and with Thy cross illumined the ends of the world, do Thou enlighten with the light of Thy divine knowledge the hearts of those who rightfully hymn Thee.

The Great Shepherd of the sheep and Lord the Jews have put to death on the tree of the cross, but as sheep hath He the dead, buried in the hades, delivered from the power of death.

With Thy cross, O my Saviour, having proclaimed the glad tidings of peace and announced unto the captives their release, Thou hast, O Christ, put to shame him that was in power, by Thy divine rising shewing his naked destitution.

[*The Theotokion.*]

The supplications of those that faithfully pray, O all-hymned, do not despise; but rather accept and convey them unto Thy Son, O purest, unto God the sole Benefactor, for in thee we have acquired a protectress.

Another, the Heirmos: Being the God of peace...

O the riches and the depths of the wisdom of God! The Lord that keepeth the worldly-wise hath made us free from their wiles; for having voluntarily suffered in the feebleness of flesh, by His life giving strength hath He raised the dead.

Christ being God, uniteth Himself with flesh for our sake, and is crucified, dieth and is buried, and riseth again and ascendeth up with His own flesh to the Father; therewith also will He come again and save those that serve Him piously.

The Theotokion:

O pure Virgin, holy of holies, that didst bring forth the Holy One of the holy, Who sanctifieth all, even Christ the Redeemer; wherefore we proclaim thee, Queen and Sovereign of all, as Mother of the Maker of all things created.

Another, the Heirmos: Thou that hast enlightened with the brightness...

Delighted are the powers of the heavens beholding thee; with them rejoice also the assemblies of men; for they became united through thy bringing forth, O Virgin Theotokos, which we worthily glorify.

Let all the tongues of men and their thoughts be directed unto the laudation of the true ornament of men: the Virgin is clearly present glorifying those who in faith hymn her wonders.

Worthy of praise is every hymn of the wise and all laudation that are offered unto the Virgin and Mother of God; for she whom we worthily glorify hath been the temple of glory of the Most High God.

Ode 6. *The Heirmos:*

An extreme abyss hath surrounded us, there is no one that can deliver, we are accounted as sheep for slaughter! O save Thy people, our God, for Thou art the might and restoration of the feeble.

By the stumbling of the first fashioned we were terribly wounded, but were healed by Thy wound with which Thou, O Christ, wast, for our sake, afflicted; for Thou art the might and restoration of the feeble.

Thou hast led us up out of the hades, O Lord, having slain the all-devouring whale and with Thy might, O all-powerful, having destroyed his strength; for Thou art life and light and the resurrection. [*The Theotokion.*]

In thee, O purest Virgin, are rejoicing the first progenitors of our race, having regained through thee the Eden which they ruined with their transgression; for thou art pure, both before bearing and after bringing forth.

Another, The Heirmos: Out of the belly Jonah...

Being a mind impassible and immaterial, Christ the God mingleth Himself unto the human mind, through the medium of the divine nature and the grossness of the flesh, and without mutation uniteth Himself entirely unto the whole of my being, so as to grant unto me, the fallen one, in my entirety the salvation by His crucifixion.

Being tempted Adam falleth and entrapped is sore afflicted, having been anciently frustrated in his hope of deification; but he riseth up deified in the union of the Word and through the passion attaineth impassivity, on the throne is glorified as the Son that sitteth together with the Father and the Spirit.

[*The Theotokion*].

The God that reigneth rightfully, without quitting the bosom of the Unoriginate Begetter, in the bosom of a pure maiden establisheth Himself, and, formerly motherless, becometh incarnate without father; His awful generation is without genealogy and ineffable.

Another, The Heirmos: An extreme abyss hath surrounded us...

Thy confinement are as slaves attending the heavenly ranks, rightfully wondering at thy seedless birth, O Ever-virgin; for thou art pure, both before bearing and after giving birth.

Incarnate of thee, O purest, hath become the Word, formerly incorporeal, that maketh all things by His will, having brought from non-existence the troops of the bodiless, as all powerful.

Slain was the enemy by thy life-bearing fruit, thou full of God's grace, and manifestly trodden under foot was the hades and we that were chained obtained our deliverance; wherefore I cry out: Destroy the passions of my heart.

The Contakion, Tone 1, *similar to:* When thou comest...

Thou hast risen as Lord from the tomb and hast withal revivified the world, consequently human nature hymneth Thee as God and death hath vanished, whereas Adam is jubilant, O Master, and Eve, being now freed from fetters, rejoiceth crying: Thou art He that grantest, O Christ, resurrection unto all.

The Oikos:

Let us hymn as God all-powerful Him Who rose again the third day and the gates of the Hades shattered, and raised from the grave those that were therein from beginning, Who in His own good pleasure appeared to the myrrh-bearing women, having first said to these, Hail, commanded them to announce gladness to the Apostles, as the sole Life-giver; wherefore in faith the women proclaim unto the disciples the symbols of victory, the hades groaneth and the death bitterly weepeth, whereas the world is joyful and all things rejoice therewith; for thou, O Christ, hast granted unto all the resurrection.

Ode 7. *The Heirmos:*

Thee, O Theotokos, as an intellectual furnace do we, the faithful, contemplate; for just as the Most Exalted One hath saved the three youths, the whole world did He in thy womb renew, the God of the fathers, laudable and most glorious.

Frightened was the earth, the sun hidden and the light enveloped in darkness, torn became the divine veil of the Temple, and the rocks were rent; for on the cross was hanging the Just One, God of the fathers, laudable and most glorious.

Having voluntarily and for our sake found Thyself as helpless and wounded among the dead, Thou, O most Exalted One, hast set all free, and with Thy mighty arm raised together with Thee, O God of the fathers, laudable and most glorious. [*The Theotokion.*]

Hail, thou source of ever-living water, hail, thou paradise of delicacies, hail, thou bulwark of the faithful; hail, thou that knewest no marital life, hail, thou gladness of all the world through whom unto us shone forth the God of the fathers, laudable and most glorious.

Another, The Heirmos: The youths to the piety...

As of old accurst was the earth, having been dyed with the blood of Abel, by the fratricidal hand*; so it is blessed now by being besprinkled with the flow of Thy divine blood, and leaping for joy crieth out: O God of the fathers, blessed art Thou.

May the God-opposing people of the Jews bewail the effrontery of putting Christ to death, but let the Gentiles rejoice, let them clap their hands and call out: O God of the fathers, blessed art Thou.

---

* Genesis 4, 8.

Behold, resplendently shining before the myrrh-bearing women an angel called out unto them: Come and see the symbols of the resurrection of Christ—the shroud and the grave, and cry aloud: O God of the fathers, blessed art Thou.

Another, The Heirmos: Thee, O Theotokos, as an intellectual...

Thee, O Theotokos, as a ladder doth Jacob prophetically perceive *; for through thee the Most Exalted One appeared upon the earth, and had His abode among men as He was pleased, the God of the fathers, laudable and most glorious.

Hail, O pure one, for out of thee came forth the Shepherd Who in clothing Himself with Adam's skin, hath truly, the Most Exalted One, put on the whole of me, the man, through His incomprehensible tenderness of heart, the God of the fathers, laudable and most glorious.

A new Adam from thy pure blood hath the Ever-existing God truly become; Him now supplicate to renew me, the decayed one, who calleth out: O God of the fathers, laudable and most glorious.

Ode 8. *The Heirmos:*

In the furnace as in a forge did the youths of Israel shine with the beauty of piety purer than gold, saying: Bless the Lord, all ye the works of the Lord hymn and exalt Him unto all the ages.

Thee Who by Thy will every thing maketh and transformeth, Who hath with Thy passion the shadow of death turned into life everlasting, O Word of God, Thee unceasingly do we, with all the works of the Lord, hymn as Lord and exalt unto all the ages.

Thou, O Christ, hast put an end to the destruction and misery within the gates and bulwarks of the hades, having risen from the grave on the third day; Thee unceasingly hymn as Lord all the works and exalt unto all the ages. [*The Theotokion:*]

Her that hath, without seed and supernaturally from the divine flesh, brought forth the very precious pearl, Christ, let us

---

* Genesis 28, 12, 13.

hymn, saying: Bless the Lord, all ye the works of the Lord, hymn and exalt Him unto all the ages.

Another, The Heirmos: Of supernatural wonder...

Come, O ye people, let us adore the place on which stood the spotless feet *, and whereon Christ's divine and life-giving palms were stretched out on the tree for the salvation of all men, and drawing around the grave of life, let us sing: May every created thing bless the Lord and exalt Him unto all the ages.

Convicted hath become the wicked calumny of the God-slaying Jews; for He Whom they called a deceiver, rose up as a Powerful One, having made a mockery of their senseless seals †. Wherefore rejoicing let us sing: May every created thing bless the Lord and exalt Him unto all the ages. [*Of the Trinity:*]

In thrice Holy theologizing the glory of one Lordship ‡, the spotless Seraphim, with fear and as slaves, glorify the three-hypostatical Godhead §; with them let us also piously sing: May every created thing bless the Lord and exalt Him unto all the ages.

Another, The Heirmos: In the furnace as in a forge did the youths of Israel...

The resplendent bridal chamber out of which came Christ the Master of all as a bridegroom, let us all hymn, singing: All ye the works of the Lord hymn the Lord and exalt Him unto all the ages.

Hail, thou glorious throne of God; hail, thou of the faithful the wall through which shone forth the light, Christ, unto those that were in darkness and that glorify thee and cry aloud: O all ye the works of the Lord hymn the Lord and exalt Him unto all the ages.

Having brought forth unto us the Lord—the cause of salvation, supplicate, O all-hymned Virgin, for all of us who diligently cry aloud: Bless the Lord all ye the works of the Lord, sing and exalt Him unto all the ages.

---

* Psalm 131, 7. † Matth. 27, 67. ‡ Of one Lordship. § Isaiah 6, 3.

Thereupon we sing the hymn of the Theotokos: My soul doth magnify the Lord...*with the refrain:* More honourable than the Cherubim...

Ode 9. *The Heirmos.*

A type of thy chaste birth proved to be the burning-bush that was not consumed; do extinguish, we entreat thee, the furnace of temptations which is even now raging within us, that we may, O Theotokos, unceasingly magnify thee.

O how the lawless and mutinous people that have plotted evil, set free the proud and impious man, whereas they condemned to be hung on the tree, the Just One, the Lord of glory, Whom we properly magnify*.

O Saviour, the blameless Lamb that hast taken away the sins of the world†, Thee together with the Father and Thy Divine Spirit we glorify as the One risen on the third day and the Lord of glory; Him theologizing we magnify. [*The Theotokion:*]

Save Thy people, O Lord, whom Thou hast purchased with Thy precious blood, granting strength unto the Emperor against his enemies and unto Thy churches giving peace, O Lover of man, through the intercessions of the Theotokos.

Another, the Heirmos: The strange mystery...

Celebrated hath become Thy cross, O Lord, by Thine ineffable might, for Thy weakness hath shown itself unto all as above might: therewith the mighty were brought down to earth and the lowly are led up to heaven‡.

Slain is the death detested by us, for having appeared to those in the hades, Thou, O Christ, hast through the resurrection from the dead granted life§; therefore in hymns Thee, as Life and Resurrection and Light hypostatical, we magnify.

[*Of the Trinity:*]

Unoriginate and infinite nature becometh known in three single hypostaces of divine origin as one Godhead in the

---

* John 18, 39. † John 1, 29; Isaiah 53, 7 and 4. ‡ I Corinth 1, 25; Luke 1, 53. § For resurrection from the dead Thou, O Christ, hast granted on Thine appearing to those in the hades.

Father and the Son and the Holy Spirit, thereon trusting the godly-wise Emperor is saved.

Another, the Heirmos: A type of thy chaste...

From David's root—the prophetic and God-parental—hast thou sprung, O Virgin, but even David hast thou truly glorified having borne the prophesied God of glory, Whom we properly magnify.

Every law of eulogies is triumphed over by the majesty of thy glory, O purest one, but, O Sovereign Lady, deign to accept the laudatory hymn which is being lovingly and fervently offered unto Thee, O Theotokos, by thine unworthy servants.

O the wonders of thine that pass all understanding! for thou, O Virgin, alone and clearer than the sun, hast given unto all to comprehend the newest wonder, O purest, of thine incomprehensible birth; wherefore we all magnify thee.

The little ectene. Thereupon: Holy is the Lord our God...*thrice*

The matutinal Exaposteilarion. With Lauds the Sticheras of the resurrection, Tone 1.

We hymn Thine, O Christ, saving passion and glorify Thy resurrection.

Thou that hast endured the cross, made death void and risen from the dead, O Lord, make our life peaceful as the only One All-powerful.

Thou that hast spoiled the hades and raised up man by Thy resurrection, O Christ, make us worthy, in purity of heart, to hymn and glorify Thee.

Glorifying Thy God-befitting condescension, we hymn Thee, O Christ: of a virgin wast Thou born, yet wast not separated from the Father; Thou hast suffered as man and of free will endured the cross; Thou hast risen again from the grave going forth as from a bridal chamber, that Thou mayest save the world,—O Lord, glory to Thee.

Other, Oriental Sticheras, the same Tone:

When Thou wast nailed to the tree of the cross, then the might of the enemy was slain, the creation shook with fear of

Thee and the hades was spoiled by Thy might; Thou hast raised the dead from their graves and unto the malefactor opened the paradise; O Christ, our God, glory to Thee.

The honourable women with lamentations diligently worked their way unto Thy tomb, but found the grave opened, and having heard from the angel the new and most glorious wonder, announced unto the apostles that the Lord is risen granting unto the world great mercy.

We bow down both before the divine sores of Thy passion, O Christ the God, and before the Lord's sacrifice in Zion that took place at the end of the ages and manifested God, for upon those that were sleeping in darkness the Sun of righteousness hath shined, leading them unto the never setting light; O Lord, glory to Thee.

O ye, tumultuous race of the Jews, suggest where are those who came to Pilate? Let the soldiers that were watching say: Where the seals of the sepulchre are? Whither was transferred the Buried One? Where was sold the Unsaleable One? How was the Treasure stolen? Why do ye calumniate the Saviour's rising, O most lawless Jews? Risen is the free One among the dead and granteth unto the world great mercy.

Glory... The matutinal Stichera of the Gospel. Both now...

Exceedingly blessed art thou, O Theotokos Virgin; for through Him that was incarnate of thee is the hades made captive, Adam recalled, the curse became void, Eve set free, death slain and we are restored to life. Wherefore in hymns we cry aloud: Blessed art Thou, O Christ the God, Who thus hast been well pleased; glory to Thee.

The Great Doxology. Thereupon the Troparion of the resurrection.

To-day is salvation come unto the world; let us sing to Him that arose from the grave and is the author of our life, for having by death destroyed death, He hath given us the victory and the great mercy. *And the dismission.*

In the Liturgy, at the Tipics, with the Beatitudes, Tone 1.

By eating hath the enemy led Adam out of the paradise, and by cross hath Christ led therein the malefactor, who was calling: Remember me, when Thou comest in Thy Kingdom.*

I adore Thy passion, I doxologize also the resurrection, with Adam and the malefactor in a joyful tone I cry aloud unto Thee: Remember me, O Lord, when Thou comest in Thy Kingdom.

Crucified wast Thou, O Sinless One, and wast voluntarily laid in a tomb, but hast risen again as God, awakening with Thee Adam calling: Remember me, when Thou comest in Thy Kingdom.

Thy temple of the body having raised by Thy three days' sepulture, together with Adam hast Thou, O Christ the God, raised also the offspring of Adam crying: Remember us, when Thou comest in Thy Kingdom.

The myrrh-bearing women very early came weeping to Thy tomb, O Christ the God, and found an angel sitting in white raiments, who called out: What seek ye? Risen is Christ, henceforth weep not.

Thine Apostles, O Lord, having come into the mountain where Thou hadst appointed them,† and seen Thee, O Saviour, worshipped Thee; these hast Thou sent also unto the nations to teach and to baptize them.

Glory...of the Trinity.

Let us all together adore the Father, and doxologize the Son, and hymn the All-holy Spirit, calling out and saying: O All-holy Trinity, save us all. [*Both now...*

Thy people, O Christ, bring before Thee Thy Mother as a supplicant; through her pleadings grant unto us, O Good One, Thy compassions that we may glorify Thee, Who didst shine forth unto us from the grave.

---

* Luke, 23, 42. † Matth. 28, 16.

The Prokeimenon, Tone 1.

Let Thy mercy, O Lord, be upon us as we have put our hope in Thee.

The verse: Rejoice in the Lord, O ye righteous; praise becometh the upright (*Psalm* 32, 22. 1).

Alleluia: It is God Who giveth vengeance to me, and subdueth peoples under me.

The verse: He magnifieth the salvations of the King and dealeth mercifully unto His Christ, unto David and his seed for evermore (*Psalm* 17, 48 *and* 51).

ON SATURDAY, AT THE GREAT VESPERS.

For "O Lord I have cried" the Sticheras of the resurrection, Tone 2.

O come, let us adore God the Word that was born of the Father before ages and was incarnate of the Virgin Mary; for having endured the cross, He was buried as He Himself willed it, and having risen from the dead, He saved me the erring man.

Christ, our Saviour, having nailed to the cross the writing against us, blotted it out and abolished the power of death; we adore His resurrection on the third day.

With Archangels let us hymn the resurrection of Christ, for He is the Redeemer and Saviour of our souls and is coming again, in fearful glory and mighty power, to judge the world, which He hath fashioned.

Other Sticheras, Anatolian, Tone the same.

Thee, crucified and buried, the angel declared to be Master and said to the women: Come and see where the Lord was lying*; for He is risen, as He also Himself said, being All-powerful. Wherefore we bow down before Thee, the only Immortal One; O Christ, Giver of life, have mercy on us.

---

* Matth. 28, 6.

Upon Thy cross hast Thou made void the curse that was of the tree; in Thy grave hast Thou slain the power of death and with Thine awaking hast Thou enlightened the race of men. Wherefore we cry out unto Thee: O Christ, our God and Benefactor, glory to Thee.

Through fear were thrown open before Thee, O Lord, the gates of death and the gatekeepers of the hades were terrified at the sight of Thee, for Thou hast smashed the brazen gates and crushed the iron posts and led us out of the darkness and the shadow of death and burst our chains.

Singing the hymn of salvation, with our lips let us call out; O come ye all, let us fall down in the house of the Lord, saying: O Thou crucified on the tree and risen from the dead and abiding in the bosom of the Father—do cleanse our sins.

Both now... The Theotokion:

Disappeared the shadow of the law when the grace was come; for as the bush was not consumed, although burning, so as virgin didst thou bring forth and remain virgin; instead of pillar of fire there arose the Sun of righteousness; in place of Moses—Christ, the Salvation of our souls.

For Versicles the Sticheras of the resurrection, Tone 2.

Thy resurrection, O Christ the Saviour, hath enlightened the whole universe, and Thou hast called Thine own creatures; O Lord All-powerful, glory to Thee.

Other Sticheras in alphabetical order:

By tree, O Saviour, hast Thou made void the curse that was of the tree, the power of death hast Thou slain in Thy sepulture, and with Thine awaking hast Thou enlightened our race. Wherefore we cry out unto Thee: O Christ, our God, the Lifegiver, glory to Thee.

Having appeared nailed to the cross, Thou hast, O Christ, altered the beauty of Thy creatures; wherefore also the soldiers, showing their inhumanity, have pierced Thy side with a lance, and the Hebrews ignorant of Thy power prayed that Thy grave might be sealed; but, O Lord, Who through the mercy of Thy compassions didst accept the sepulture and hast risen again on the third day, glory to Thee.

O Christ, the Life-giver, Thou didst voluntarily endure passion for the sake of mortals, and having as Powerful gone down into the hades and rescued as from a strong* beast† those that were there waiting for Thy coming, hast paradise to live in, instead of the hades, granted unto them; vouchsafe therefore also unto us, glorifying Thine awaking on the third day, expiation of our sins and the great mercy.

Glory...Both now...The Theotokion:

O new wonder—the greatest of all the ancient wonders! For who ever had known a mother that, without a husband, hath brought forth and in her arms carried Him Who holdeth all creation? God's good will is this offspring. Him as infant having, O purest, carried in thine arms and towards Him possessing motherly boldness, do not cease to entreat Him for those who venerate thee that our souls may be commiserated with and saved. [*The Troparion of the Resurrection, Tone* 2.]

When Thou didst condescend unto death, O Life immortal, then didst Thou slay hades with the lightning flash of Thy Godhead. And when Thou hast also raised the dead from the nethermost parts, all the powers of the heavens cried out: O Life-giver, Christ, our God, glory to Thee. [*The Theotokion:*]

All beyond comprehension, all exceedingly glorious are thy mysteries, O Theotokos: sealed in purity and preserved in virginity, a true Mother art thou acknowledged, having born the true God, Him supplicate that our souls may be saved.

In the Matins after the 1*st Stichologia, the Cathismata of the resurrection, Tone* 2.

The noble Joseph, having taken down from the tree Thy purest body and having wrapped it in fine linen and covered it with spices, placed it in a new sepulchre‡; but Thou hast risen

---

* Matth. 12, 29. † From a strong hand. ‡ The Troparia of the Great Friday.

on the third day, O Lord, granting unto the world great mercy.

Unto the myrrh-bearing women presenting himself at the tomb the angel cried out: Unguents are suitable for the dead only, whereas Christ appeared a stranger to corruption; but call aloud: Risen is the Lord, granting unto the world a great mercy. *Glory...Both now...The Theotokion:*

Most blessed art thou, O Theotokos-virgin, we hymn thee; for by thy Son's cross the hades was overthrown and the death slain; having been put to death, we rose again and were made worthy of life, again obtained the paradise—that ancient delight. Wherefore, whilst giving thanks, we doxologize as Supreme Ruler Christ our God and the only One plenteous in mercy.

After the 2nd Stichologia the Cathismata, Tone 2.

Having not prevented the stone of the sepulture to be sealed, the stone of the faith hast Thou, on Thy resurrection, granted unto all, O Lord, glory to Thee.

Of Thy disciples the choir, together with the myrrh-bearing women are in one accord rejoicing; for the feast common to them all do we celebrate unto the glory and honour of Thy resurrection and, through them, cry out unto Thee: O Lord—Lover of man, grant unto Thy people a great mercy.

Glory...Both now...The Theotokion:

Exceedingly blessed art thou, O Theotokos Virgin...(*page* 19).

After "The blameless" the Hypakoe, Tone 2:

The women who after the passion came unto the sepulchre to anoint Thy body, O Christ the God, saw angels in the grave and were frightened; for they heard from them that the Lord hath risen, granting unto the world a great mercy.

The Graduals, Tone 2. Antiphon 1.

Unto the heavens I lift up the eyes of my heart, unto Thee, O Saviour; O save me by Thine illumination.*

---

* Psalm 122, 1.

Have mercy upon us who every hour commit many faults* against Thee, O my Christ, and accord me the means, before the end, to repent unto Thee. *Glory...*

Unto the Holy Spirit it behoveth to reign, to sanctify, to quicken the creature; for He is God of one substance with the Father and the Son.

Both now...the same. Antiphon, Tone 2.

If the Lord had not been on our side, who would be able to preserve himself uninjured by the enemy that is withal man-slayer also.†

For a prey to their teeth do not, O Saviour, give over Thy servant; ‡ for in the same manner as a lion mine enemies rise up against me. *Glory...*

Unto the Holy Spirit appertain both the origin of life and its honour, for everything created doth He, as God, the Existing One, preserve by power§ in the Father through the Son.

Both now...the same. Antiphon 3.

Those that trust in the Lord have become like unto the holy mount: they in no wise are moved by the assaults of the enemy.||

Unto iniquity let not the righteous put forth their hands; for Christ doth not suffer the rod upon His lot.¶ *Glory...*

Of the Holy Spirit is shed all wisdom: hence grace unto Apostles, Martyrs are crowned with sufferings and Prophets see.

Both now...the same. The Prokeimenon, Tone 2.

Arise, O Lord, my God, according to the injunction that Thou hast decreed, and the congregation of the people shall compass Thee about.

The verse: O Lord, my God, in Thee have I put my trust, save me (*Psalm* 7, 2).

---

* Psalm 122, 3. † Psalm 123, 1 and 2. ‡ Psalm 123, 6.
§ Strengthen. || Psalm 124, 1. ¶ Psalm 124, 3.

The Canon of the resurrection. Ode 1. *Tone* 2. *The Heirmos:*

In the depth did once the all-beweaponed power lay low the entire host of Pharaoh, and the Incarnate Word hath utterly destroyed the all-mischievous sin, most glorious is the Lord, for gloriously hath He triumphed.

The Prince of the world with whom we were enrolled, after disobeying Thy commandment, O Good One, was condemned by Thy cross, for he hath attacked Thee as a mortal, and fell under the might of Thy power and had his impotence exposed.

As deliverer of the race of men and prince of the incorruptible life didst Thou come into the world, for with Thy resurrection, which we all doxologize, Thou hast torn to pieces the shrouds of death; for gloriously hath He triumphed.

[*The Theotokion:*] Incomparably higher hast thou appeared, O pure Ever-virgin, than any invisible or visible creature, for the Creator hast thou brought forth, as He was pleased to be incarnate in thy womb; Him then with boldness entreat that He may save our souls.

Another Canon of the cross and resurrection. Ode 1. *Tone* 2. *The Heirmos.*

Along the unbeaten, unused track of the sea dry-shod having passed, Israel the elect cried out: Unto the Lord let us sing, for He is glorified.

Strength of the infirm, resurrection of the fallen and incorruptibility of the dead hast Thou become, O Christ, through the suffering of Thy body; for He is glorified.

Take pity on the fallen and raise up the shattered image, O God the Creator and Renovator, Thou Who having been put to death, hast restored all to life; for He is glorified.

Another Canon to the All-holy Theotokos. Tone 2. *The same Heirmos.*

An immaterial ladder of old and a strangely dried-up way of the sea have shewn forth thy birth, O pure one, which we all hymn, for He is glorified.

The Power of the Highest perfect, Hypostatis, God's Wisdom,

being incarnate of thee, O purest, held converse with men*, for He is glorified.

Through the inaccessible door of thy closed womb, O pure one, did the Sun of righteousness pass and unto the world appear, for He is glorified.

The Catabasis: I will open my mouth. *Ode* 3. *The Heirmos.*

As a lily hath blossomed up the desert—barren church of the gentiles through Thy coming, O Lord, wherein is also my heart firmly established.

At Thy passion the very creation did change, beholding Thee in the vile garb treated of the lawless with contemptuous derision, Who hast founded all by Thy divine beckoning.

Out of dust in the image with Thine own hand didst Thou fashion me, and whilst I have crumbled again into dust of death on account of sin, Thou, O Christ, having descended into the hades, hast together with Thee raised me up. [*The Theotokion* :]

The angelic orders were, O purest, astonished and the hearts of men were terrified at thy bringing forth, wherefore we in faith venerate thee as Theotokos.

Another, the Heirmos :

The bow of the mighty was shattered by Thy power, O Christ, and with strength are girded the feeble.

He that is the highest of all—Christ, by His passion in the flesh became a little lower than the angelic nature†.

Among the lawless accounted as dead, shining with the crown of glory unto the women hast Thou, O Christ, appeared at Thy resurrection.

Another, the same Heirmos :

He that is above all time as the Creator of times, out of thee, O Virgin, by his own free will a babe hath been fashioned.

The womb that is wider than the heavens let us hymn, whereby Adam rejoicing in the heavens liveth.

Ode 4. *The Heirmos :*

Of the Virgin camest Thou neither a mediator nor an angel, but Thyself—the Lord incarnate, and savedst the whole of my humanity‡; wherefore I call unto Thee: glory to Thy power, O Lord.

---

* Drew nigh unto. † Psalm 8, 6. ‡ Isaiah 63, 9.

Before the tribunal as a criminal standest Thou, O my God, without vociferating, O Master, to call down upon the nations judgment; whereby through Thy passion, O Christ, Thou hast wrought salvation unto the universe.

Through Thy passion, O Christ, the weapons of the enemy were exhausted, and with Thy descent into the hades, the cities of the adversaries were destroyed,* and the audacity of the tyrant was laid low.

The Theotokion:

As a haven of salvation and a wall unassailable, we all the faithful know thee, O Theotokos Sovereign-Lady, for by thine intercession thou deliverest from dangers our souls.

Another, the Heirmos:

I have heard, O Lord, Thy glorious œconomy and glorified, O Lover of man, Thine incomprehensible might.

Seeing Thee, O Christ, nailed to the tree, the Virgin that had painlessly brought Thee forth, suffered motherly anguish.

Vanquished is death, the Dead One doth capture the gates of the hades; for the all-devourer having been despoiled, all that is above nature hath been bestowed upon me.

Another, the same Heirmos:

Behold, exalted above the powers is the divine mountain in the house of the Lord, the God's Mother most clearly.

Having alone, outside the laws of nature, brought forth the Master of all creation, thou, O Virgin, wast made worthy of godly appellation.

Ode 5. *The Heirmos:*

Mediator between God and men wast Thou, O Christ the God,† for it is through Thee, O Master, that out of the night of ignorance we attain admission unto the source of light, Thy Father.

As cedars hast Thou, O Christ, voluntarily broken up the rage of the nations, O Master, since Thou hast been pleased to be

---

* Psalm 9, 7. † I Timoth. 2, 5.

in flesh elevated on the cypress, the pine, and the cedar trees.*

In a nethermost pit have they laid Thee, O Christ, as dead having no breath; but having with Thine own sore touched those that were forgotten, asleep in their graves, Thou raisedst them together with Thee.† [*The Theotokion.*]

Entreat thy Son and Lord, O pure Virgin, to grant peace unto those that trust in thee, unto the captives deliverance from inimical surroundings.

Another, the Heirmos:

Unto Isaiah there appeared a coal, unto those that were straying in darkness out of a virgin's womb there shone forth a Sun, bestowing enlightenment of the knowledge of God.

Refusing to be abstemious, the first man tasted of the mortiferous tree, but the second, being crucified, extinguisheth the sin of the other.

In Thy human nature liable to suffering and death wast Thou Who art impassible in Thine immaterial Godhead, and having made the dead incorruptible, Thou raisedst them, O Christ, from the nethermost parts of the hades.

Another, the same Heirmos:

O ye clouds of the joy, sprinkle sweetness unto those that are on earth, for a Child is given that existed before the ages—the Incarnate of the Virgin, our God.

Unto my life and body the light shone forth and the decrepitude of the sin hath destroyed the Highest Who in these last days was seedlessly incarnate of the Virgin.

Ode 6. *The Heirmos:*

In the abyss of sins wallowing, I call unto the abyss of Thine unfathomable mercy: out of corruption do bring me up, O God.

As a malefactor Thou, Just One, wast adjudged and along with the lawless wast nailed to the tree, granting remission unto the guilty through Thine own blood.

---

* Psalms 28, 5, and 36, 35; Isaiah 60, 13. † Psalm 87, 7, 6.

As by one man, the first Adam, the death came of old into the world, so by one also—the Son of God—the resurrection was manifested*. [*The Theotokion:*]

Without knowing a man thou, O Virgin, hast brought forth and remaineth Virgin for ever, thus showing forth the symbols of the true Godhead of thy Son and God.

Another, the Heirmos:

The sound of thanksgiving prayers that proceed from mine distressed soul hearing, do deliver me, O Master, from the cruel tormentors, for Thou art the only source of our salvation.

As custodians of the tree of life against the fallen one Thou hadst set the Cherubim, but on seeing Thee, the doors were opened, for Thou wast come making the way into paradise unto the malefactor.

Deserted is the hades and was overthrown by the death of One; for of all the riches it did possess, Christ alone, for the sake of us all, despoiled it.

Another, the same Heirmos:

Human nature enslaved to sin, through thee, O pure one—Sovereign Lady, obtained liberty; for thy Son as a Lamb was immolated for all.

We all cry out unto thee—the true Mother of God—deliver the servants that have excited anger, for thou alone possessest boldness before thy Son.

The Contakion, Tone 2:

Thou hast risen from the tomb, O All-powerful Saviour, and the hades, beholding the marvel, was terrified, and the dead rose again; whilst the creation at the sight thereof participateth in Thy joy, and Adam joineth in exultation, and the world, O my Saviour, hymneth Thee for ever. [*The Oikos:*]

Thou art the light unto those that are in darkness, Thou art the resurrection and the life of all men and Thou hast raised with Thee all, having, O Saviour, despoiled the power of death, and having, O Word, shattered the gates of the hades; and be-

---

* Rom. 5, 12; I Corinth. 15, 21 and 22.

holding the marvel, the dead were wondering and every created being participateth in the joy for Thy resurrection, O Lover of man; wherefore we all both glorify and hymn Thy condescension, and the world, O my Saviour, hymneth Thee for ever.

Ode 7. The Heirmos:

The God-repugnant command of the wicked tyrant hath caused the flames to rise up high in the air; but unto the God-honouring youths the dew of the Spirit hath stretched out Christ—the Existing One Who is blessed and most glorious.

On account of compassion wouldest Thou not endure, O Master, to see man being tortured by death, but camest and savedst him with Thine own blood, having become man, Thou the Existing One Who art blessed and most glorious, the God of our fathers.

Seeing Thee, O Christ, arrayed in garment of vengeance, the door-keepers of the hades were terrified, for Thou, O Master, wast come to slay the mad tyrant-ungrateful servant; Thou the Existing One that art blessed and most glorious, the God of our fathers. [*The Theotokion:*]

Among holy the holiest we account thee as the only one that hast brought forth the God immutable, O Virgin unpolluted, Mother unmarried, for unto all the faithful hast thou shed incorruptibility by thy divine birth.

Another, the Heirmos:

The youths of old appeared as the most eloquent philosophers, for blessing in their God-pleasing souls, with their mouths they sung: O most divine God of the fathers and ours, blessed art Thou.

Disobedience hath of old condemned the ancestor in Eden, but Thou wast voluntarily judged, absolving the transgressor of his sin, O most divine God of the fathers and most glorious.

Thou hast saved him who, in consequence of the envy of the manslayer, was wounded in the tongue through the voluntary bite in Eden, for with Thy voluntary passion* hast Thou cured him, O most divine God of the fathers and most glorious.

[*The Theotokion:*]

* In the tongue in Eden, for the voluntary bite hast Thou cured with Thy voluntary passion.

Whilst I was living in the shadow of death, Thou hast called me unto the light, having surrounded the tenebrific hades with the splendour of the Divinity, O most divine God of the fathers and most glorious.

Another, the same Heirmos :

In the night as in an enigma did Jacob behold the God incarnate, but out of thee hath He appeared in all clearness unto those that sing: O most divine God of the fathers and most glorious.

Wrestleth with Jacob,* foretokening the symbols of the ineffable intermingling in thee, O pure one, whereat was voluntarily united unto men, the most divine God of the fathers and most glorious.

An abomination is he who does not profess the Son of thee, O Virgin, as one of the All-hymned Trinity, in an undoubted conception and expression crying out: O most divine God of the fathers and most glorious.

Ode 8. *The Heirmos :*

A fiery furnace did once in Babylon divide its effects, whilst by divine command it burnt the Chaldeans with the flames and refreshed the faithful that sung : Bless the Lord, all ye works of the Lord.

Seeing the garment of Thy body purpled with Thy blood, O Christ, the angelic orders were terrified to trembling before Thy manifold long-suffering and called out: Bless the Lord, all ye works of the Lord.

Thou, O Bountiful, hast clothed my mortality with immortality by Thine awaking, wherefore, being gladdened, gratefully hymneth Thee, O Christ, Thine elect people, calling out unto Thee: Swallowed up indeed is the death by victory. [*The Theotokion :*]

Him that is inseparable from the Father and in the womb dwelled as God and man, didst thou seedlessly conceive and ineffably bring forth, O most pure parent of God; that is why as the salvation of us all we acknowledge thee.

---

* Genesis, 32, 24.

Another, The Heirmos :

Disdaining the golden image and seeing the unchanging and living image of God, the thrice-blessed youths, in the midst of the fire, loudly sung: Let all creation sing unto the Lord and exalt Him unto all the ages.

To the cross being nailed wast seen Thou that art rich in mercy, voluntarily wast Thou buried and hast risen again on the third day, and hast redeemed, O Lover of man, all those that in faith sing: Let all creation hymn the Lord and extol Him unto all the ages.

To deliver from the corruption him whom Thou, O Christ, hadst fashioned by Thy divine might, Thou, O Word of God, hast descended into the nethermost parts, and having granted him incorruptibility, Thou hast made him a partaker of Thine eternal glory, that all creation vociferating may hymn and exalt Christ unto the ages.

Another, The same Heirmos :

Through thee was seen on earth and with men hath dwelled He that is incomparable in goodness and might; and singing unto Him we all the faithful call out: Let all the realized creation hymn the Lord and exalt Him unto all the ages.

In proclaiming thee as truly pure one, we glorify the Theotokos, for thou hast brought forth the Incarnate One of the Trinity, unto Whom with the Father and the Spirit we all sing: Let all creation hymn the Lord and exalt Him unto all the ages.

Ode 9. *The Heirmos.*

Of the unoriginate Father the Son, God and Lord, being incarnate of the Virgin, hath appeared unto us to enlighten those that are in darkness and to gather together the dispersed, wherefore we magnify the all-hymned Theotokos.

As in Eden, so planted on the Calvary the thrice-rich tree of Thine, O Saviour, undefiled cross, being watered with the divine blood and water as from a source from Thy divine side, O Christ, hath germinated life for us.

Being crucified, O all-powerful, Thou hast laid low the mighty, and exalting that part of humanity which was lying below in the stronghold of the hades, on the Father's throne hast Thou placed it; worshipping Thee coming therewith we magnify Thee. *[Of the Trinity.]*

Unity of three numbers, Trinity of one substance let us, O faithful, glorify by hymning in the orthodox way—that indivisible most divine Substance, thrice resplendent, never darkening Evening-light, the only incorruptible, that hath shed forth light unto us.

Another, the Heirmos: Of God God the Word...

In the midst of the condemned, as a Lamb having been lifted up on Calvary upon the Cross, having Thy side, O Christ, pierced with a lance, life hast Thou as Good One granted unto us—the earthy—that in faith honour Thy divine resurrection.

The God that by His own death hath mightily abolished the dominion of death let us all the faithful adore, for He hath raised with Him those that died ages before and unto all giveth life and resurrection.

Another, the Heirmos:

Wholly art Thou, O Lord, the desire, entirely the sweetness, O Word of God, Son of the Virgin, God of Gods, Holiest of the holy; wherefore we all magnify Thee with her that bare Thee.

As staff of strength the Word of God was given in thy womb, O pure one, unto the frail nature, which, even though it hath slid into the hades, He had raised; wherefore thee, O purest, as Theotokos do we magnify.

Her whom Thou, O Master, hast selected, do mercifully accept Thy mother as an intercessory for us, and the whole universe will be full of Thy bounty, so that we all may magnify Thee as Benefactor.

With the Lauds the sticheras of the resurrection, Tone 2.

Every breath and every creature doth glorify Thee, O Lord, for with Thy cross Thou hast abolished death that Thou shouldest shew unto the peoples, as the sole Lover of man, Thy resurrection from the dead.

Let the Jews tell how the soldiers destroyed the King whilst guarding Him ? Why then the stone did not preserve the Rock of life ? Let them either give up the Buried One, or adore the Risen One, saying together with us: Glory unto the multitude of Thy mercies, our Saviour; glory to Thee.

Be glad, O ye people, and rejoice. The Angel that was sitting on the tomb-stone, he announced to us the glad-tidings: Christ is risen from the dead, the Saviour of the world, and hath filled everything with sweet smell. Be glad, O ye people, and rejoice.

Angel it was that before Thy conception, O Lord, unto the one full of grace had brought "Hail" as greeting, Angel also hath rolled the stone off Thy glorious tomb at Thy resurrection, that one, in the place of sorrow, was announcing the symbols of joy, and this other, instead of death, was proclaiming unto us the life-giving Master; wherefore we cry out unto Thee: O Lord, Benefactor of all, glory to Thee.

Other Oriental Sticheras, Tone 2.

With lamentations did the women pour out the perfumes over Thy tomb, and their mouth was filled with joy when it was said: Risen is the Lord.

Let nations and peoples laud Christ, our God, Who voluntarily did for our sake suffer the cross and spend three days in the hades, and let them adore His resurrection from the dead, whereby all the ends of the world became enlightened.

Crucified and buried wast Thou, O Christ, as Thou willedst, Thou hast overthrown death and risen again in glory as God and Master, granting unto the world life eternal and great mercy.

O ye truly wicked that in sealing the tomb-stone vouchsafed unto us greater wonders! The watchmen bring the intelligence: This day hath He departed from the grave, and ye told them: Say that, whilst we were asleep, His disciples came and stole Him. But who would steal a dead body and still less a naked one? He Himself hath risen again by His own power as God, having left in the tomb His funereal belongings. Come, behold, O ye Jews, He did not break the seals, Who hath overcome death and unto the race of men granted an endless life and great mercy.

After the Great Doxology, the Troparion:

Being risen from the tomb and having burst the bonds of hades, Thou hast, O Lord, loosed the condemnation of death, delivering all from the snares of the enemy; and manifesting Thyself to Thine apostles, Thou didst send them forth to preach and through them hast granted Thy peace to the universe, O only plenteous in mercy.

In the Liturgy with the Beatitudes, Tone 2.

The cry of the malefactor we bring unto Thee and pray: Remember us, O Saviour, in Thy Kingdom.

We bring unto Thee for the remission of sins the cross which Thou for our sake hast taken, as Lover of man.

We adore Thine, O Master, burial and resurrection wherewith Thou hast delivered the world from corruption, as Lover of man.

By Thy death, O Lord, was death swallowed up, and through Thy resurrection, O Saviour, hast Thou saved the world.

The myrrh-bearing women hast Thou met, on rising from the grave, and unto Thy disciples hast enjoined to tell of Thy resurrection.

Those that were sleeping in darkness in the nethermost parts of the hades have risen on beholding, O Christ, Thee, the Light.

Glory...

Let us all glorify the Father, adore the Son and faithfully hymn the Holy Spirit.

Both now...The Theotokion:

Hail thou—the fiery throne, hail—the bride unmarried, hail—thou, O Virgin, that God unto the men hast brought forth.

The Prokeimenon, Tone 2.

The Lord is my strength and my song and is become my salvation.

The Verse: Sorely hath chastened me the Lord, but He did not give me over unto death (*Psalm cxvii,* 14. 18).

Alleluia: May the Lord hearken unto thee in the day of tribulation; may the name of the God of Jacob shield thee.

The Verse: O Lord, save the king and hearken to us in what day soever we shall call upon Thee (*Psalm xix,* 2. 10).

ON SATURDAY, AT THE GREAT VESPERS.

For "O Lord, I have cried" the Sticheras of the resurrection, Tone 3.

By Thy cross, O Christ the Saviour, the dominion of death hath been broken down and the devil's enchantment dispelled; and the race of men, being saved by faith, doth constantly bring a hymn unto Thee.

Enlightened have become all things through Thy resurrection, O Lord, and the paradise is open once more; and the whole creation acclaiming Thee doth constantly bring a hymn unto Thee.

I glorify of the Father and of the Son the power, and I hymn the authority of the Holy Spirit, the indivisible, non-created God-head, the Trinity consubstantial, reigning for ever.

Other, Anatolian Sticheras, the same Tone:

Thy honoured cross, O Christ, we adore, and Thy resurrection we hymn and glorify, for through Thy wound we all were healed.

We hymn the Saviour incarnate of the virgin, for for our sake was He crucified and rose again on the third day, granting unto us a great mercy.

Having come down unto those that were in the hades, Christ announced the glad tidings, saying: Be reassured, I have conquered now; I am the resurrection, I shall lead you up, having destroyed the gates of death.

Unworthily standing in Thine undefiled house, we send up the vespertine hymn, deeply crying unto Thee, O Christ the

God: Do Thou, that hast enlightened the world with Thy resurrection on the third day, tear away Thy people from the hand of Thine enemies, O Lover of man.

Glory...Both now...the Theotokion:

How can we help wondering at thy theandric birth, O most highly honoured one, for, without having had marital intercourse, thou, O spotless one, hast without father brought forth in flesh a Son, that before ages was born of a Father without mother, and that in no way hath undergone either any change, or intermingling or division, but preserved in their entirety the peculiarities of each substance: wherefore, O virgin-mother, Sovereign Lady, do entreat Him that may be saved the souls of those who rightfully confess thee as Theotokos.

For Versicles the Sticheras of the resurrection, Tone 3.

Do Thou, O Christ, Who with Thy passion hast darkened the sun and with the light of Thy resurrection illumined all things, accept our vespertine hymn, O Lover of man.

In alphabetical order:

Thy life-bearing awaking, O Lord, hath enlightened the whole universe and reclaimed Thy ruined creation; wherefore, having been delivered from Adam's curse, we cry out: O all powerful Lord, glory to Thee.

Being God immutable, Thou hast undergone a change whilst suffering in flesh; the creation, unable to bear the sight of Thee hanging, was bowed down with fear and bemoaning, and hymneth Thy long suffering; and, having descended into the hades, Thou hast risen on the third day, giving to the world life and great mercy.

That Thou mayest deliver our race from death, Thou hast, O Christ, suffered death; and, rising on the third day from the dead, Thou hast raised together with Thee those who have acknowledged Thee as God, and hast enlightened the world; O Lord, glory to Thee.

Glory...Both now...the Theotokion:

Without seed, of the Divine Spirit, and by the will of the Father, didst thou conceive the Son of God that before the ages was of the Father without mother, Him also Who for our sake was of thee without Father, hast thou in flesh brought forth, and as a babe hath suckled with thy milk; wherefore cease not to intercede that our souls may be delivered from perils.

The Troparion of the resurrection, Tone 3.

Let those of heaven rejoice, and may those of earth exult, for the Lord hath wrought might with His arm; He hath by death trampled upon death, hath become the first begotten of the dead;* He hath delivered us from the belly of the hades and granted to the world great mercy.

Glory...Both now...the Theotokion.

Thee that wast the mediator of the salvation of our race do we hymn, O Theotokos-Virgin, for in the flesh taken from thee thy Son and our God, having deigned to endure the passion of the cross, hath redeemed us from corruption as the Lover of man.

At the Matins, after the 1*st Stichologia, the Cathismata of the resurrection, Tone* 3.

Christ is risen from the dead; as the first fruits of them that slept, the first begotten of every creature† and the Creator of all things, He hath in Himself renewed the corrupted nature of our race; no longer then, O death, canst thou lord it over, for the Master of all hath destroyed thy dominion.

In flesh having tasted of death, Thou hast, O Lord, done away with the bitterness of death in Thine own awaking, and hast strengthened the man against it, having revoked the mastery of the first curse; O Lord, Protector of our life, glory to Thee.

---

* Coloss. 1, 18. † 1 Corinth. 15, 20; Coloss. 1, 15.

Glory...Both now...the Theotokion.

Awed by the beauty of thy virginity and by thy brightest purity, Gabriel called out unto thee, O Theotokos: What encomium worthy of thee can I bring unto thee? and what name shall I apply to thee? I am struck with amazement and fear; wherefore do I call out unto thee as I was told: Hail, thou full of grace.

After the 2nd Stichologia, the Cathismata of the resurrection, Tone 3.

Terrified by Thine immutable divinity, and by Thy voluntary passion, O Lord, the hades was inwardly bewailing: I tremble before the uncorrupted hypostasis of the body.* I behold the Unseen One that is secretly fighting against me, wherefore those also whom I hold cry out: Glory, O Christ, to Thy resurrection.

We, the faithful, theologize the ineffable mystery—the incomprehensible one of the crucifixion and the inexplicable one of the awaking, for to-day both the death and the hades were despoiled, and the human race hath put on incorruption; wherefore gratefully do we call out unto Thee: Glory, O Christ, to Thine awaking.

Glory...Both now...the Theotokion:

The incomprehensible and uncircumscribable One, of the same substance with the Father and the Spirit hast thou mysteriously contained in thy womb, O God's Mother; and the one and unmingled energy of the Trinity, we have learned, through thy birth, to glorify in the world; wherefore and in giving thanks we call out unto thee: Hail, thou full of grace.

After "the Blameless," the Hypakoi, Tone 3.

Astounding by his appearance, refreshing by his speech, the radiant angel said unto the myrrh-bearing women: Why seek ye the Living One in the tomb? Risen is He that hath emptied the graves; know Him as the immutable Changer of corruption; say

* The bodily uncorrupted compound.

unto God: How fearful are Thy works, for Thou hast saved the human race!

The Graduals, Tone 3. *The Antiphon* 1*st, each verse being repeated:*

The captivity of Zion* hast Thou brought out of Babylon, draw me also from passions unto life, O Word.

In the South, those that sow in divine tears, reap ears in the gladness of eternal life.†

Glory...

Unto the Holy Spirit, just as unto the Father and the Son, is reflected together every good gift, in Whom every thing liveth and moveth.

Both now, the same. The Antiphon 2nd:

Except the Lord build the house of virtues, in vain do we labour, and when He protecteth our souls, no one shall destroy our city.‡

Of the fruit of the womb by the Spirit made sons unto Thee, O Christ, just as unto the Father, the saints ever are. *Glory...*

Of the Holy Spirit is inspired every holy thing, wisdom, for He realizeth every creature; unto Him let us serve, for He is God, just as unto the Father and the Word.

Both now...the same. The Antiphon 3rd:

Blessed are those that fear the Lord, that walk in the way of His commandments, for they shall eat of every living fruit.§

Rejoice, O Chief-Shepherd, seeing round about Thy table Thine offspring,‖ carrying branches of good works. *Glory...*

Of the Holy Spirit cometh every abundance of glory, of Him also the grace and the life of every creature, for He is hymned together with the Father and the Word.¶

---

* Psalm 125, 1. † Psalm 125, 4 and 5. ‡ Psalm 126, 1. § Psalm 126, 3. ‖ Psalm 127, 1 and 2. ¶ Psalm 127, 4.

Both now... The Prokeimenon, Tone 3.

Say among the nations that the Lord is enthroned, for He hath established the universe which shall not be moved.

The Verse: O sing unto the Lord a new song. (*Psalm* 95, 10 *and* 1).

The Canon of the resurrection. Tone 3. *Ode* 1. *The Heirmos:*

He that by a divine sign hath of old united the waters into one whole, and divided the sea unto the people of Israel, This same our God is most glorious, unto Him alone we sing, for He is glorified.

He that hath condemned the earth to bring forth unto the transgressor thorns as the fruit of his sweat,* a crown of thorns from the lawless hand having received in flesh, This same our God hath made the curse void, for He is glorified.

Vanquisher and Master of death hath become He Whom the death hath smitten, for having taken impassioned living flesh and wrestled with the enemy, This same our God hath raised with Him all, for He is glorified.

The Theotokion:

As Theotokos indeed all nations glorify thee that hast brought forth without seed, for having come down into thy sanctified womb, This same our God, that was realized after us, both God and man was born of thee.

Another Canon of the cross and resurrection. Tone 3. *Ode* 1.

The Heirmos: Let us, O people, intone a new melody...

The race of man that was enslaved by the tyrant enamoured of sin, Christ hath redeemed with divine blood, and having deified it hath renewed it, for He is glorified.

As mortal desirous of death, the Treasurer of life, even Christ, hath tasted thereof, but being immortal in His substance, He hath revived the dead, for He is glorified.

---

* Gen. 3, 18-19.

Another Canon of the all-holy Theotokos. Tone 3. *Ode* 1, *the same Heirmos :*

Before Him that was incarnate of thee, O Virgin, doth with due propriety bow the knee every creature in heaven, together with those both on earth and under the earth,* for He is glorified.

O what reconciliations have taken place in thee ! for He that so abundantly bestoweth all good things, having, as God, given us the Divine Spirit, hath taken flesh from thee, O Maiden, for He is glorified.

The Catabasis : I will open my mouth...

Ode 3. *The Heirmos :*

Thou that out of nothing hast produced everything which was fashioned by the Word and accomplished by the Spirit,† O Master of the universe, in Thy love do stablish me.

By Thy cross, the wicked one was put to shame, for, having finished the pit which he dug, he himself fell into it, and the horn of the humble was exalted in Thy resurrection, O Christ.

The preaching of piety unto the nations hath as water covered the seas, O Lover of man ; for having risen from the grave, Thou hast revealed the light of the Trinity.

The Theotokion :

Glorious things were spoken of thee, the living city of One that ever reigneth,‡ for through thee, O Sovereign Lady, God hath dwelled together with those of earth.

Another, the Heirmos : Bow of the enemy hast Thou broken...

Purifier of the abominations of idols hast thou, undefiled cross, proved to be, for Jesus, the most divine, hath spread upon thee His arms.

May we all the faithful adore thee, O life-bearing tomb ; for in thee was laid and rose again Christ, our very God.

---

* Philip. 2, 10. † Psalm 32, 6. ‡ Psalm 86, 3.

Another, the same Heirmos:

A rod of the root of Jesse, the Virgin, as was prophesied, having sprouted forth, Thou, O Christ, as a flower didst shine unto us; holy art Thou, O Lord.

That Thou mayest make the earthborn partakers of the divine, Thou hast impoverished Thyself in taking our flesh from the virgin; Holy art Thou, O Lord.

Ode 4. The Heirmos:

A firm love hast Thou set to us-ward, O Lord, for Thine Only-begotten Son hast Thou given unto death for us;* wherefore we gratefully cry out unto Thee: Glory to Thy power, O Lord.

Sores and wounds hast Thou, O Lord, compassionately taken up with, bearing the injury of the blows against Thy cheeks and long-sufferingly enduring the spitting into Thy face, wherewith hast Thou achieved my salvation: Glory to Thy power, O Lord.

In Thy mortal body hast Thou, O Life, partaken of death, for the comfortless trouble's sake of the needy and because of the deep sighing of Thy poor; and, having spoilt the seducer, Thou didst, O most glorious One, raise with Thee all, for Thou art glorified.†

The Theotokion:

Be mindful, O Christ, of the flock which Thou hast bought with Thy passion; of Thy most blessed Mother compassionate entreaties accepting and visiting the afflicted, do Thou deliver by Thy power, O Lord.

Another, the Heirmos: A strange and ineffable...

Having created man in Thine image, Thou, O Lover of man, when he was slain by sin on account of the transgression, hast saved him by being crucified on the calvary.

The dead that were swallowed up, death hath given back, and the pernicious dominion of the hades was destroyed, when Thou rose again from the grave, O Lord.

---

* Joh. 3, 16. † Psalm 11 6.

The Theotokion:

O Mary, pure art thou, and a golden censer! for having, without mingling, as One of the Trinity, come down into thee, the Incarnate God the Word hath filled the world with sweet odours.

Another, the same Heirmos:

Thou, O Master, that by the measure of the divine knowledge hast fixed mountains, art the Stone without hands cut out of the Virgin; glory to Thy power, O Lover of Man.

Our diseased nature hast Thou re-established, O Master, having in the Virgin united thereunto as the most efficacious remedy Thine, O purest Word, Divinity.

My portion and most desired heritage art Thou, O Lord, that hast, through the Virgin, united me, O Word, unto Thy hypostasis, having in flesh been hypostasis.

Ode 5. *The Heirmos:*

I watch early unto Thee—the Creator of all things, the peace that passeth all understanding, for a light are Thy commandments, do guide me therein.

Having been, through the envy of the Jews, delivered unto an iniquitous judge and judging righteously all the earth, Thou that seest all, hast delivered Adam from the ancient condemnation.

Thy peace unto Thy churches by the invincible power of Thy cross, O Christ, that art risen from the dead, do grant and save our souls.

The Theotokion:

A holy tabernacle, and more ample than the heavens, thou alone hast appeared, O Ever-Virgin, since thou didst receive the Word of God that could not be contained in all the creation.

Another, the Heirmos:

Upon the earth hast Thou, Invisible One, appeared and voluntarily dwelled together with men, O Incomprehensible One, and keeping early watch for Thee we hymn Thee, O Lover of man.

With a lance in Thy side having been pierced, O my Christ, Thou didst her that was formed from man's side and was instrumental in bringing about the ruin unto all men, deliver from the curse.

Being in substance equal with the Father, the holy temple of Thy purest and most venerable body hast Thou, O Christ our Saviour, raised from the dead.

Another, the same Heirmos :

The Word of God—thy Son, O Virgin, the Creator of Adam the first created is not a creature, notwithstanding that He did fashion for Himself out of thee a living flesh.

Equal with the Father is thy Son, O Virgin, the Word of God, perfect hypostasis in two natures, Jesus the Lord, both perfect God and man.

Ode 6. *The Heirmos :*

The greatest abyss of sins hath encompassed me and my spirit abandoneth me ; but, O Master, stretching out Thy sublime arm, do Thou, O Pilot, save me, as Peter.

An abyss of mercy and compassions hath encompassed me through Thy tender-hearted coming down, for having become incarnate and been in the form of a servant Thou, O Master, hast deified and glorified me together with Thee.

The slayer hath undergone destruction, on seeing the slain one resuscitated; of Thy resurrection, O Christ, these are the symbols and of Thine undefiled passion the prize.

The Theotokion :

O purest, thou that above all understanding alone wast the intermediary between the Creator and the human race, do entreat that thy Son be merciful unto thy sinful servants, and be a protector unto them.

Another, the Heirmos :

Having been a natural type of One dwelling in the nethermost hades, Jonah cried out : Out of corruption lead up my life, O Lover of man.

Having Thyself suffered sores, by the passion of Thy cross hast Thou raised together with Thee from the hades those that were wounded. Wherefore I call unto Thee: Out of corruption lead up my life, O Lover of man.

Through fear the gates of the hades became opened before Thee, O Christ, and the enemy's belongings ravished; wherefore Thou wast met by the women that heard gladness instead of sorrow.

Another, the same Heirmos:

A form like unto ours assumeth from the uncorrupted Maiden, He that is foreign to any shape, and becometh both of the form and substance a man, without changing the Divinity.

From the abyss of sins and the tempest of passions do deliver me, O purest, for thou art a haven and an abyss of wonders for those that in faith flee unto thee.

The Contakion, Tone 3. *Similar to:* The Virgin to-day...

Thou didst this day rise from the tomb, O merciful One, and hast led us up from the gates of death; to-day Adam exulteth and Eve rejoiceth, and conjointly with them the prophets and the patriarchs unceasingly hymn the godly might of Thy power.

The Oikos:

Let the heaven and the earth exult this day and with one accord hymn Christ the God, for he hath raised from the graves those that were chained. The whole creation rejoiceth also, bringing unto the Creator of all and our Deliverer songs worthy of Him, for this day He, as Life-giver, having led up with him from the hades men, doth exalt them with Him to heaven, and doth put down the arrogance of the enemy and destroyeth the gates of the hades by the divine power of His authority.

Ode 7. *The Heirmos:*

As of old the three pious youths hast Thou refreshed with the dew in the Chaldean flame, so do illuminate with the bright fire of the divinity us also that are calling out unto Thee: Blessed art Thou, O God of our fathers.

Rent in twain was the bright veil of the temple at the crucifixion of the Creator, manifesting thereby the truth hidden in the scripture unto the faithful that call out unto Thee: Blessed art Thou, O God of our fathers.

Thy side being pierced, with the drops of Thy divine life-giving blood, O Christ, that were providentially falling down on the earth, Thou hast restored those of the earth that call out unto Thee: Blessed art Thou, O God of our fathers. [*Of the Trinity.*]

The Good Spirit, together with the Father and the Son, the Only-begotten, let us, O faithful, glorify, whilst venerating in the Three one origin and one God-head, and calling out: Blessed art Thou, O God of our fathers.

Another, the Heirmos:

Conceited was the tyrant, yet a plaything proved to be for the children, for as dust having trodden the seven-fold heated flames, they sung: Blessed art Thou, O Lord, the God of our fathers.

The sun was darkened—not on account of an ordinary man hanging on the cross, but beholding God incarnate, unto Whom we also sing: Blessed art Thou, O Lord, the God of our fathers.

Having received the One strong in His Godhead, Granter of incorruption, the timorous hades hath vomited out the souls of the righteous that were crying out: Blessed art Thou, O Lord, the God of our fathers.

The Theotokion:

Thou hast, O purest, appeared as a precious treasury of blessings unto those that with pure hearts confess thee as God's Mother, for of thee was incarnate the God of our fathers.

Another, the same Heirmos:

Thou, the Lord of glory and Dominator of the higher powers, Thou that ever sittest together with the Father, and wast carried in virginal arms, blessed art Thou, O Lord, the God of our fathers.

Audacious is the death, but him holding converse with Thee hast Thou destroyed, having become God-hypostatical flesh from the Virgin; blessed art Thou, O Lord, the God of our fathers.

We all have learned thee to be Theotokos that barest the God, for thou hast brought forth One of the Trinity Who was incarnate of thee; blessed is, O purest, the fruit of thy womb.

Ode 8. *The Heirmos:*

Before the unbearable fire standing together, but remaining unscathed of the flame, the God-fearing youths sing this divine hymn: Bless the Lord, all ye the works of the Lord, and exalt Him unto all the ages.

Rent in twain was the temple's brightness, when Thy cross was set up on the calvary, and the creation was bowing down with fear and chanting: Bless the Lord, all ye the works of the Lord, sing and exalt Him unto all the ages.

Risen art Thou, O Christ, from the grave, and by Thy divine power through the tree hast restored the one fallen through temptation, who calleth out saying: Bless the Lord, all ye the works of the Lord, sing and exalt Him unto all the ages.

The Theotokion:

God's temple wast thou become, a living repository and ark, for thou, O God's purest parent, hast conciliated the Creator unto men, and worthily do we, all the works, hymn thee and extol unto all the ages.

Another, the Heirmos:

The flame of material fire have the God-beholden youths withered with the immaterial one, and sung: Bless the Lord, all ye the works of the Lord.

The Word is not passible, for in the Divinity it is impassible, and it was in the flesh that God hath suffered, to Whom also we psalmodize: Bless the Lord, all ye the works of the Lord, hymn and exalt Him unto all the ages.

Having fallen asleep as a mortal, Thou, O Saviour, hast risen again as immortal one, and dost deliver from death those that cry unto Thee: Bless the Lord, all ye the works of the Lord, hymn and exalt Him unto all the ages. [*Of the Trinity:*]

We serve piously unto the three-hypostatic Godhead, ineffably united, and sing: Bless the Lord, all ye the works of the Lord, hymn and exalt Him unto all the ages.

Another, the same Heirmos :

The intellectual orders hast thou surpassed as Mother, and wast near God; we bless, O blessed Virgin, thy bringing forth and extol unto all the ages.

The beauty of nature hast thou made appear more beautiful, shining forth the divine flesh; we bless, O blessed Virgin, thy bringing forth and extol unto all the ages.

Ode 9. The Heirmos.

A new and God-becoming wonder; for through the closed door of the Virgin there visibly passeth the Lord, naked on entering and flesh-bearing at the coming forth the God hath appeared, and the door remaineth closed; her that is ineffably the Mother of God, we magnify.

Terrible it is, O Word of God, to behold Thee, the Maker, elevated on the tree, and God in the flesh suffering for His servants, lying without breath in the grave, and yet delivering the dead from the hades; wherefore Thee, O Christ, as All-powerful, we magnify.

From the corruption of death hast Thou, O Christ, saved our ancestors, having been laid as dead in the grave, and a life wast Thou blossomed forth that raised the dead, brought the human nature unto the light and clothed it with divine incorruption. Therefore Thee as an Ever-living Source of light we magnify. [*The Theotokion :*]

Temple and throne of God hast thou appeared wherein was settled He that dwelleth on high, that was born without thine O purest, knowing a man, and of thy flesh did in no way open the door; therefore by thine, O honoured one, incessant entreaties do quickly and finally bring the tribes of the heathen under our Emperor.

Another, the Heirmos :

Struck with the sweet arrow of thy most pure bringing forth and admiring thine, O honoured one, covetable beauty, in angelic hymns do we worthily magnify thee as the Mother of God.

From the ignominious death hast Thou made honour to flow unto all men, for having, O Saviour, tasted thereof in Thy crucifixion, with Thy mortal substance hast Thou granted unto me, O Christ, incorruption, as Lover of man.

Thou hast saved me, having risen from the grave, O Christ, Thou hast elevated me and brought unto the Father, Thy Begetter, and seated together with Thee on the right hand, for the sake of Thy compassionate mercy, O Lord.

Another, the same Heirmos:

For the pious faithful there can never be enough of laudation in honour of thee, O Virgin, for experiencing ever-increasing divine and spiritual desire, as Mother of God do we continually magnify thee.

Thou hast appointed for us, O Christ, an unfailing interceder in her that bare Thee; for the sake of her entreaties Thou grantest us propitious Spirit, the Giver of goodness, Who proceedeth from the Father through Thee.

For the Lauds the Sticheras of the resurrection, Tone 3.

Come all ye nations, learn the power of the awful mystery; for Christ, our Saviour, that is the Word from the beginning, for our sake was crucified and voluntarily suffered burial, and rose up from the dead that He may save all things; Him let us adore.

Thy custodians, O Lord, have declared all the wonders; but the frivolous council have filled their hands with money, thinking thus to conceal Thy resurrection which the world doth glory; have mercy on us.

With joy everything was filled on learning the proof of the resurrection, for Mary Magdalene, coming to the tomb, found an angel, in resplendent apparel, sitting on the stone and saying: Why seek ye the Living One among the dead? He is not here, but is risen, as He had said, telling you thereof beforehand in Galilee.

In Thy light, O Master, we shall see the light, O Lover of man: for Thou hast risen from the dead, granting salvation unto the race of man, so that the whole creation may doxologize Thee the only Sinless One; have mercy on us.

A matutinal hymn the myrrh-bearing women were with tears bringing unto Thee, O Lord, for having sweet-smelling spices they reached Thy tomb that they may anoint Thine all-purest body. An angel sitting on the stone hath declared unto them: Why seek ye the Living One among the dead? for having trodden upon death He is risen as God, granting unto all a great mercy.

A shining angel over Thy life-giving tomb said unto the myrrh-bearing women: The Redeemer hath emptied the graves, despoiled the hades and rose again on the third day as the Only God and All-powerful.

In Thy tomb Mary Magdalene was looking for Thee, having come there on one of the sabbaths, and finding Thee not, with lamentations was crying out: Woe me, O my Saviour! stolen hast Thou been, O King of all. And a couple of life-bearing angels from within the sepulchre called out: Why, woman, weepest thou? I weep, she said, because they have taken my Lord from the grave, and I know not where they have laid Him. And turning back, she called out, as soon as she perceived Thee: O my Lord and my God, glory to Thee.

The Hebrews have shut up in the tomb the Life, and the malefactor hath with his tongue opened the delight, calling out and saying: He that for my sake was crucified with me, did hang on the tree by my side and hath appeared unto me on the throne sitting with the Father; for He is Christ, our God, having a great mercy.

In the Liturgy with the Beatitudes, Tone 3.

Our forefather Adam who rejected Thy commandment, Thou, O Christ, hast driven out of the paradise, and the malefactor, that confessed Thee on the cross, hast Thou, O Compassionate One, settled therein, since he called out: Remember me, O Saviour, in Thy Kingdom.

For our sins hast Thou, O Life-giver and Lord, condemned us unto the curse of death, and having in Thy body, O Sinless Master, suffered, Thou hast awakened the dead calling out: Remember us also in Thy Kingdom.

Having risen from the dead, through Thy resurrection, O Lord, Thou hast delivered us from sufferings, and the whole dominion of death hast Thou, O Saviour, destroyed. Therefore we in faith call out unto Thee: Remember us also in Thy Kingdom.

By Thy three days burial, having as God resuscitated those that were slain in the hades, Thou hast raised them together with Thee, and hast caused, O Good One, incorruption to flow unto us all that in faith ever call out: Remember us also in Thy Kingdom.

Unto the myrrh-bearing women first hast Thou appeared, O Saviour, on Thy rising from the dead, and called out: Rejoice, and through these Thou, O Christ, dost announce Thy resurrection unto Thy friends, wherefore in faith we call out unto Thee: Remember us also in Thy Kingdom.

Spreading out on the mount his arms, Moses hath typified the cross and obtained victory over the Amalekites; and we in faith taking it up as a strong weapon against demons, all call out: Remember us also in Thy Kingdom. *Glory...*

Let us, O faithful, hymn the Father, Son and Holy Spirit, One God, One Lord, as from one sun, for the Trinity is a Three-shining Light and enlighteneth all those that call out: Remember us also in Thy Kingdom. *Both now...*

Hail thou, the divine door through which the Creator hath passed at His incarnation, having preserved it sealed; hail—the light-cloud, the divine rain bearing Christ; hail—the ladder and heavenly throne; hail—the divine mount, venerated, fertile, unbroken.

The Prokeimenon:

O sing praises unto our God, O sing praises, O sing praises unto our King, O sing praises.

O clap your hands, all ye nations, shout unto God with the voice of gladness (*Psalm* 46, 7. 1).

Alleluia: In Thee, O Lord, have I put my trust, let me never be ashamed.

The Verse: Be Thou unto me as God Protector and a House of refuge in order to save me (*Psalm* 30, 2-3).

ON SATURDAY, AT THE GREAT VESPERS.

For "O Lord, I have cried," the Sticheras of the resurrection, Tone 4.

Thy life-giving cross, O Christ the God, incessantly adoring, we glorify Thy resurrection on the third day, for therewith hast Thou, O All-powerful, renewed the corrupted human nature, and pointed out to us anew the ascent into heaven, as the only Good One and Lover of man.

The penance for the disobedience respecting the tree hast Thou, O Saviour, remitted, having been voluntarily nailed to the tree of the cross, and having descended into the hades, as All-powerful One, the fetters of death hast Thou, as God, broken; wherefore we adore Thy resurrection from the dead, joyfully crying out: O All-powerful Lord, glory to Thee.

The gates of the hades hast Thou, O Lord, shattered and with thy death the kingdom of death hast Thou demolished, and the race of man hast delivered from corruption, granting unto the world life, incorruption and great mercy.

Other Sticheras, the composition of Anatolius:

Come, O people, let us hymn the rising of the Saviour on the third day, whereby we were delivered from the unbreakable chains of the hades and have all obtained incorruption and life, calling: Thou that wast crucified, buried and risen, save us by Thy resurrection, O only Lover of man.

Angels and men hymn, O Saviour, Thine awaking on the third day whereby were enlightened the ends of the universe and we all were delivered from the thraldom of the enemy, calling: O Vivifier, All-powerful Saviour, save us by Thy resurrection as the only Lover of man.

The gates of brass hast Thou shattered and the door posts destroyed, O Christ the God, and the fallen human race hast Thou raised. Wherefore in harmony do we cry aloud: Thou that art risen from the dead, O Lord, glory to Thee.

O Lord, Thy being begotten of the Father is eternal and everlasting, Thine incarnation of the Virgin is for men unutterable and inexplicable, and Thy descent into the hades is terrible for the devil and his angels; for, having trodden upon death, Thou hast risen on the third day, granting unto men incorruption and great mercy.

Glory...Both now...the Theotokion:

The Prophet David, that through thee hath become God's ancestor, did in melody declare concerning thee unto Him that hath done great things unto thee: Upon Thy right hand there stood the Queen*, for thee as Mother, cause of life, hath shewn the God Who was pleased without Father to become incarnate of thee that He might renew again His image ruined by passions, and having found amid dangerous mountains the straying sheep and taken it upon His shoulder, He might bring it unto His Father and, in accordance with His own device, unite it unto the heavenly † powers, and save, O Theotokos, the world,—even Christ, that hath great and abundant mercy.

For Versicles the Sticheras of the resurrection, Tone 4.

O Lord! having ascended the cross, Thou hast annulled our ancestral curse, and having descended into the hades, Thou hast set free those that were for centuries imprisoned therein, granting incorruption unto the human race; wherefore in hymns we glorify Thy vivifying and saving awaking.

Other Sticheras in their alphabetical order.

Being hung on the tree, O Only Powerful, Thou hast shaken the whole creation, and being laid in the grave, Thou hast raised those that dwell in the graves, granting incorruption and life unto the human race. Wherefore in hymns we glorify Thine awaking on the third day.

The lawless people have handed Thee, O Christ, over to Pilate, condemned Thee to be crucified, thus proving ingratitude unto their Benefactor; but voluntarily hast Thou suffered the

---

* Psalm 44, 10. † Luke 15, 45.

burial, by Thine absolute power hast Thou risen again on the third day as God, granting unto us life everlasting and great mercy.

With tears having reached the tomb, the women were looking for Thee and finding Thee not, wept bitterly and loudly lamenting said: Woe unto us, our Saviour, the King of all—how wast Thou stolen? and what receptacle doth hold Thy life-bearing body? And an angel replying unto them, saith: Weep not, but going about preach ye that risen is the Lord Who granteth us joy, as the only Compassionate One.

Glory... Both now... the Theotokion:

Look down upon the entreaties of thy servants, O all spotless one, putting an end to the terrible attacks against us, freeing us from every affliction, for in thee we have the only sure and certain anchor and thine intercession we have acquired. Let us not be put to shame, O Sovereign-Lady, who call upon thee; do hasten unto prayer for those that in faith cry aloud unto thee: Hail, O Sovereign-Lady, thou the help of all, joy and shelter and salvation of our souls.

The Troparion, Tone 4:

Having learned from the angel the glorious message of the resurrection, and thrown off the ancestral sentence, the women-disciples of the Lord exultingly spake to the apostles: Spoiled is death, Christ the God is risen, granting to the world great mercy.

Glory ... Both now... the Theotokion:

The mystery hidden from eternity and unknown to the Angels, is through thee, O Theotokos, manifested to those on earth, God, by union without confusion, being incarnate of thee, and having of His own will deigned to endure for us the cross, therewith raising the first-fashioned, He hath saved our souls from death.

At the Matins, after the 1*st Stichologia the Cathismata of the resurrection. Tone* 4.

Beholding the entrance to the sepulchre and being unable to bear the flaming brightness of the angel, the myrrh-bearing women were amazed and tremblingly said: Hath He been stolen that had opened paradise unto the malefactor? Is He risen that, before even His passion, preached of His awaking? Truly risen is Christ, granting unto those in the hades life and resurrection.

Of Thine own free deliberation hast Thou, O Saviour, suffered the cross; and in a new grave mortal men have laid Thee, Who, with a word, didst put together the ends (of the world); wherefore was bound the strong one, death was terribly despoiled and all those in the hades called out unto Thy life-bearing awaking: Christ is risen—the Life-giver that abideth unto the ages.

Glory ... Both now ... The Theotokion:

Wonder-struck was Joseph contemplating that which is above nature, and with respect to thy seedless conception, O Theotokos, he took into consideration the dew on the fleece, the bush that was not consumed by fire, Aaron's staff that sprouted, and bearing witness, thy betrothed and guardian called out unto the priests: Virgin giveth birth and after the birth remaineth still virgin.

After the 2*nd Stichologia, the Cathismata of the resurrection. Tone* 4.

Risen art Thou from the grave as Immortal, O Saviour; together with Thee hast Thou raised Thy world by Thy might, O Christ, our God; Thou hast broken by Thy strength the dominion of death and manifested, O merciful One, the resurrection unto all; wherefore also we glorify Thee, O only Lover of man.

From the highest regions coming down and approaching the stone whereunder was the Stone of life, white-garmented Gabriel called out unto the weeping: Leave off your cries of lamentation, since ye even now have something gracious; for—have courage! He whom ye seek is truly risen; wherefore call unto the apostles that the Lord is risen; adore the Risen One, having received gladness; take courage then, let Eve also have courage.

Glory...Both now...the Theotokion:

Wonder struck were, O pure one, all the choirs of angels at the mystery of the terrible bringing forth, how He that sustaineth all things solely by His mere beck, was as man held in thine arms, and hath taken beginning the Eternal One, and was suckled at the breast, He that in His ineffable goodness feedeth every breath, and praising thee as truly the Mother of God, they glorify thee.

After "the Blameless" the Hypakoe, Tone 4:

Concerning Thy glorious awaking, O Christ, the myrrh-bearing women, having gone before, proclaimed unto the Apostles, that Thou hast arisen, as God, granting to the world great mercy.

The Graduals, Tone 4. The first Antiphon:

From my youth up many a passion hath vexed me*, but do Thyself, O my Saviour, protect and save me.

Ye, that hate Zion, shall be confounded of the Lord, for as grass by fire, so shall ye be withered.† [*Glory...*

By the Holy Spirit every soul is quickened, and through purity elevated it is made resplendent by the triune Unity in a sacredly mysterious way.

Both now...the same. The Antiphon 2.

I have called unto Thee, O Lord, ardently from the depth of my soul, and may Thy divine ears become attention unto me.‡

He that hath acquired trust in the Lord § is higher than all that grieve.

*Glory...*By Holy Spirit are caused streams of grace which fill every creature unto vivification.

---

* Psalm 128, 1-2. † Psalm 128, 5-6. ‡ Psalm 129, 1-2. § Psalm 129, 4.

Both now...the same. The Antiphon 3.

Let my heart be lifted up unto Thee, O Word, and let nothing of the world's charms enchant me unto a weakness.*

Just as unto his mother † one hath an affection, unto the Lord we are indebted with a yet warmer love. [*Glory...*

By Holy Spirit is abundance of the knowledge of God, of contemplation and wisdom; for unto Him all the injunctions of the Father are revealed by the Word.

Both now...the same. The Prokeimenon. Tone 4.

Arise, O Lord, help us and deliver us, for Thy name's sake. *Verse:* O God, with our ears have we heard: (Psalm 43, 27. 2).

The Canon of the resurrection, a composition of John of Damascus. Ode 1. *The Heirmos:*

The red abyss of the sea with unmoistened steps having crossed on foot, the Israel of old hath through the cruciform arms of Moses obtained victory in the wilderness over the forces of Amalek.

Raised upon the undefiled tree of the cross wast Thou, O Master, repairing our falling off and healing the universal ruin through a tree, as a Good One and All-powerful.

In the tomb bodily, in hades with Thy soul as God, in paradise with the malefactor and on the throne with the Father and the Spirit wast Thou, O Christ, filling all things, O Uncircumscribed.‡

The Theotokion:

Without seed, by the will of the Father, of the Divine Spirit hast thou conceived the Son of God and in flesh brought forth Him Who is of the Father without mother and, for our sake, of thee without father.

Another Canon of the cross and resurrection. Ode I. Tone 4. *The Heirmos:* I will open my mouth and it shall be filled with the Spirit...

Thou hast, O Lord, made whole the ruined mankind, having renewed it with Thy divine blood, and hast demolished the

* Psalms 130, 1. † Psalm 130, 2. ‡ In the Hours of the Holy Pasch.

dominion of the strong one that of old had broken the work of Thy hands.

Resurrection of the dead wast Thou become through being put to death, for the power of slaying was taken away after it had wrestled with the Life Eternal, with God Incarnate that dominateth all.

The Theotokion :

More surpassingly than the heavenly powers was Thy divine living temple, even the Virgin, Thy holy mountain that carried in her womb Thee, our God.

Another Canon of the most holy Theotokos. Ode I. Tone 4. *The Heirmos :* Strong hosts He that was born of the Virgin...

People trembled, nations were agitated, and powerful kingdoms retreated, O pure one, out of fear before thy bringing forth, for my King is come and hath put down the tyrant and delivered the world from corruption.

Living on high, but coming down to men Thou hast, O Christ, sanctified Thine abode and shewn it to be steadfast, for thou that hast brought forth the Creator, after the birth alone remainedst the treasure of virginity.

Ode 3. *The Heirmos :*

Delighted on Thine account is Thy Church, O Christ, calling unto Thee : Thou art my strength, O Lord, both refuge and support.

The Tree of life, the Intellectual and True Vine is hanging on the cross, causing incorruption to flow unto all.

As a great One, as fearful, as One that hath put down the rage of the hades and as God incorruptible art Thou now risen in flesh. [*The Thetokion :*

Thou wast, O Mother of God, unto those on earth the sole intermediary for the good things that are above nature, wherefore we bring unto thee " Hail ! "

Another, the Heirmos : Thy hymnologists, O Theotokos...

The serpent hath plunged into me, O Saviour, his teeth full of poison, and these with the nails in Thy hands, O Sovereign

Almighty Lord, hast Thou broken, for there is none among the holy more holy than Thou art, O Lover of man.

Seen wast Thou, O Lover of man, as voluntarily dead in the grave, O Life-giver, and the gates of the hades hast Thou thrown open unto the souls kept therein for ages; for there is none among the holy more holy than Thou art, O Lover of man.

The Theotokion :

Unploughed furrow hast Thou appeared that did bring forth the ear of life, unto all who participate of immortality—the cause thereof, the Holy One that holily reposeth among the holy.

Another, the Heirmos : From on high hast Thou voluntarily come down on earth....

Human nature becometh purified, being through thee placed near the unbearable divine fire and like unto a mysterious bread baked in thee, O most pure Virgin, whom it also did preserve unhurt.

Who is this one that is so truly near God as to excel all the angelic orders? She is the only one that sparkleth with the beauty of virginity as Mother of the Almighty.

Ode 4. The Heirmos :

Elevated on the cross seeing Thee, the Sun of righteousness, the Church stood up in her order worthily calling out: Glory to Thy power, O Lord.

Healing up my passions, Thou hast ascended the cross with the passion of Thine undefiled flesh which Thou didst voluntarily put on; wherefore we call out unto Thee: Glory to Thy power, O Lord.

Having tasted of Thy sinless, life-giving body, death was deservedly slain, O Master; and we call out unto Thee: Glory to Thy power, O Lord.

The Theotokion :

Thou hast, O Virgin, brought forth without knowing a man and after the birth thou didst remain still a virgin; wherefore with never-ceasing voices and in undoubted faith we call out unto thee: Hail.

Another, the Heirmos : The unfathomable God's counsel...

Placed under the law Israel did not recognise in Thee, O Christ, the Law-giving God, but as a lawless one they nailed Thee to the cross, transgressing the law and proving unworthy thereof.

Thy deified Soul, O Saviour, having captured the treasures of the hades, raised together with itself the souls that were therein from the beginning, and Thy life-bearing body caused incorruption to flow unto all.

The Theotokion :

As Ever-virgin and truly Theotokos we all glorify thee, O all pure one, whom unto Moses, the Godseer, hath typified the bush that was on fire and yet remained unconsumed.

Another, the Heirmos : Sitting in glory...

Whilst living with men, seeing was the Unseen One that is in the form of the incomprehensible Godhead, and having taken the strange form from thee, O maiden, He saveth those that acknowledge thee as pure Mother of God.

The Virgin hath received in the form of matter the Immaterial One that as an infant participating of matter was of her; wherefore in two natures He is recognised as One both flesh-bearing God and man super-substantial.

He that hath settled in thee, as a virgin, and without seed was brought forth and remained Word and God, did preserve thee a virgin after the birth, just as a virgin He left thee at the birth, being Sovereign-Lord and Maker of all creation.

Ode 5. The Heirmos :

Thou, my God, didst come into the world as light, as a holy light that bringeth out of the darkness of ignorance those who in faith hymn Thee.

Thou, O Lord, compassionately camest down unto the earth; Thou didst elevate the fallen human nature, having been raised on the tree.

Thou hast taken for me the condemnation of the sins, O Christ; Thou hast made void the pains of death, O Compassionate One, with Thy divine resurrection.

The Theotokion:

Thee we bring forward as an unconquerable weapon against enemies; thee we have acquired as anchor and hope of our salvation, O God's bride.

Another, the Heirmos: Everything became frightened on account of the divine....

Infatuated hades hath with his mouth swallowed Thee whole, for seeing Thee nailed to the cross, pierced with a lance, without breath, he accounted Thee—the Living God—an ordinary mortal, but through experience he learned the strength of Thy divinity.

When the temple of Thy body, O Lover of man, was destroyed, both the grave and hades separately and involuntarily were laid under contribution : one—namely—had to give up together with Thee the souls of the saints, and the other their bodies, O Immortal One.

The Theotokion:

Behold, fulfilled is now the prediction of the prophet, for thou, O Virgin that knewest not a man, hast had in thy womb the God Who is above all, and hast brought forth the Son Eternal, Who granteth peace unto all those that hymn thee.

Another, the Heirmos: To-day I shall arise....

Having made His abode in thee, O pure one, the Son of God hath rendered thee for us a house of glory, God's holy mount, bride, bridal chamber, temple of sanctification and paradise of everlasting sweetness.

From virginal blood hast Thou, O Christ, taken the flesh without seed, most pure, hypostatic, endowed with reason and intelligence, with soul, energy, desire, self-lordship and independence.

The virginal belly hath put to shame the mind of the tyrants, for an Infant hath thoroughly probed with His hand the serpent's soul-destroying wound, and putting down the haughty traitor, hath brought him under the feet of the faithful.

Ode 6. *The Heirmos:*

I will sacrifice unto Thee, O Lord, with the voice of praise—crieth out unto Thee the Church having been cleansed of the demon's blood with the blood that mercifully run out of Thy side.

Thou hast ascended the cross, having girded Thyself with a sovereign power, and having closed with the tyrant, Thou didst, as God, hurl him down from on high and raised up Adam by Thine invincible might.

Thou didst arise, O Christ, from the tomb, shining with brilliant lustre and beautiful and hast scattered all the enemies by Thy divine might, and hast filled all things, as God,with joy.

The Theotokion:

O wonder, the newest of all wonders, that a virgin having, without knowing a man, conceived in her womb Him Who upholdeth all things, did find room therefor without a strain.

Another, the Heirmos: I have reached the depth of the sea...

The hades hath opened his pharynx and swallowed me up, and enlarged his maddened soul; but Christ having come down, brought me up alive, as Lover of man.

Death hath perished by death, for He that died, hath risen again granting me incorruption, and appearing unto the women, He announced gladness, O Immortal One.

The Theotokion.

Thy pure womb, O Theotokos, hath proved a receptacle of unendurable Godhead, whereat the heavenly orders; were unable to look without fear.

Another, the same Heirmos:

The serpent did of old entice me and hath killed me through the first mother Eve; but now, O pure one, He that fashioned me, hath through thee called me out of corruption.

The abyss of ineffable mercy hath shewn thee, O maiden, to be a select abyss of wonders, for out of thee hath shone forth in the lightning flash of divinity the Pearl—Christ.

The Contakion, Tone 4. *Similar to :* Thou hast appeared to-day...

My Saviour and Redeemer from the grave hath, as God, delivered the earthborn from the fetters and shattered the gates of hades and, as Master, hath risen on the third day. *The Oikos.*

Let us all the earth-born hymn Christ the Life-giver, that hath on the third day risen from the dead, and by His power hath to-day shattered the gates of death and slain the hades, reduced to powder the sting of death and made free Adam together with Eve,—let us sing our praise assiduously; for He, as the only powerful, God and Master, hath risen on the third day.

Ode 7. *The Heirmos :*

In the Persian furnace the youths, descendants of Abraham, burning rather with love of piety than with the flame of fire, have called out: Blessed art Thou in the temple of Thy glory, O Lord.

Washed with the divine blood of Christ, the humanity hath been called to incorruption, and in returning thanks singeth: Blessed art Thou in the temple of Thy glory, O Lord.

As vivifying, as incomparably better than paradise and truly far superior to any royal bridal chamber hath proved to be Thine, O Christ, most resplendent tomb—the source of our resurrection*.

Hail thou, the hallowed divine tabernacle of the Most High, for through thee the joy is vouchsafed to those, O Theotokos, who call out: Blessed art thou amongst women, O all spotless Sovereign-Lady*.

Another, the Heirmos: The godly-wise refused to serve creature rather than the Creator...

Elevated on the tree, Thou hast humbled the haughty eye, and the raised eye-brow hast Thou brought down to the ground, having saved the man,—O most highly hymned Lord and God of the fathers, blessed art Thou.

With Thy power do raise up the horn of us that serve Thee,

---

* In the Hours of the Holy Pasch.

O Master, Who hast risen from the dead and hast emptied the hades of her former riches—of a multitude of men,—O most highly hymned Lord and God of the fathers, blessed art Thou.

[*Of the Trinity:*

Following divine sayings, we glorify One Godhead as a flame of three lights, neither mixed up together nor interfering one with another, the eternal flame enlightening the whole creation that calleth out: O God, blessed art Thou.

Another, the Heirmos: The three youths in Babylon...

The fire of the virginal love that is in my heart constraineth me in hymns to cry out unto the Mother and Virgin: O blessed one, the Lord of hosts is with thee.

Higher than the created things hast thou appeared since thou hast brought forth the Maker and Lord; wherefore I cry out unto thee, O Theotokos: O blessed one, the Lord of hosts is with thee. [*Of the Trinity:*

Honouring Thee as One indivisible Lordship in three sanctities, I hymn three-hypostatical nature, calling out unto Thee: O blessed One, that doth govern everything.

Ode 8. *The Heirmos:*

Having spread his hands, Daniel did close the jaws of the lions in their den*; and the force of the fire was deadened † by the zealously pious youths who girded themselves with virtue and called out: Bless the Lord, all ye the works of the Lord.

Having spread Thy hands on the cross, Thou hast, O Master, gathered together all the nations and shewn one Church, hymning Thee; both those in heaven and those on earth harmoniously psalmodizing: Bless the Lord, all ye the works of the Lord, sing and exalt Him unto the ages.

Apparelled in white garments and resplendent with the unapproachable light of resurrection, there appeared unto the women an angel who cried out: Why seek ye in the grave as dead the Living One? Truly risen is Christ, unto Whom we do

---

* Dan. 6, 18. 22. † Dan. 3, 8.

cry out: All ye the works, sing unto the Lord, and exalt Him unto all the ages. [*The Theotokion:*

Thou alone in all generations wast manifested as Mother of God, O all-pure Virgin; thou wast the abode of Godhead, O all-spotless one, and wast not scorched by the fire of the unapproachable Light, wherefore we all bless thee, O Mary—God's bride.

Another, the Heirmos: The pious youths in the furnace...

Beholding Thine unrighteous immolation the creation did grow dark and sob, for whilst the earth trembled, the sun hath put on darkness as a black garment; but we unceasingly hymn Thee, O Christ, and extol unto the ages.

Having come down unto me even unto the hades, and having made the way for all in Thy resurrection, Thou hast ascended again, taking me up on Thy shoulders and bringing unto the Father*; wherefore I call unto Thee: Hymn the Lord ye works, and exalt Him unto all the ages. [*Of the Trinity:*

We glorify the first Intellect and Cause of everything, the Father, the only One without a cause, so also the Word without beginning, and the Comforting Spirit—the One God of all, adoring the Conjunct Trinity and exalting It unto all the ages.

Another, the Heirmos: The Deliverer of all, O All-powerful...

The Lord of all, that made thee of Adam's side, was incarnate of thy virginity; hymning Him we call out: Bless the Lord, all ye the works, hymn Him and exalt unto the ages.

Abraham in his tent saw the mystery that is in thee, O Theotokos, for he received thy Son without flesh and sung: Bless the Lord, all ye the works, hymn and exalt Him unto the ages.

Those that were equal in number unto the Trinity, hath saved the prefigurement of thy virginity, for in virginal bodies they have, O Maiden, trampled the flames, crying out: Bless the Lord, hymn and exalt Him unto the ages.

---

* Luke 15, 20.

Ode 9. *The Heirmos:*

A stone cut out without hands from an untouched mountain—from thee, O virgin, was separated—that corner stone,* even Christ, Who hath joined together the distant natures; rejoicing thereat we magnify thee, O Theotokos.

Thou hast taken me up entirely, but without mixture, into union with Thee, unto me all granting, O my God, the salvation through Thy passion, which Thou didst bodily endure on the cross in flesh for Thy great mercy's sake.

Thy disciples seeing Thy grave opened, and the God-worn shrouds emptied by Thy resurrection, spake together with the angel: The Lord is risen indeed.

Of the Trinity:

Adoring unity in Divine substance, but trinity in hypostases, we all the faithful now piously magnify equal power and equal honour in the unmixed hypostases.

Another, the Heirmos: Every earthborn ...

Fawningly did the serpent creep and hath carried me captive away from Eden, but against the hardest Stone of Golgotha the Lord Almighty hath dashed him as one of the little ones,† and once more opened unto me, through the tree of the cross, the entrance to the delights.

Thou hast now laid desolate the fortified strongholds of the enemy; with Thine all-powerful hand hast Thou despoiled him of all his riches, having raised me also from the ruins of the hades, and hast shewn, O Christ, him that did of old vaunt without measure, derided as ridiculous.

O come, do as Lover of man, visit the vexations of Thy humble people, and with Thy compassionate and mighty arm fortify Thy cross-bearing Emperor against the blaspheming enemy, that he may be the deliverer of Thy select inheritance, O Christ.

*** Dan. 2, 34.** **† Psalm 136, 9.**

Another, the Heirmos : The divine thing, ineffably concealed in thee ...

We see thee, O all-purest, as a lily ornamented with a purple cover of the Divine Spirit, shining in the midst of the tares and filling with sweet smell those that sincerely magnify thee.

The Incorruptible One having, out of compassion, taken unto Himself the perishable nature of man out of thy womb, O all-spotless one, hath shewn it to be imperishable with Him; wherefore as Theotokos we magnify thee.

Dominating everything created, do thou grant unto thy people the trophies of victory, making the enemy conciliatory unto the Church, that we may magnify thee as Theotokos.

With the Lauds the Sticheras of the resurrection. Tone 4.

O Lord all-powerful that hast suffered the cross and death and didst arise from the dead, we glorify Thy resurrection.

Upon Thy cross hast Thou, O Christ, delivered us from the ancient curse, and by Thy death hadst Thou suppressed the devil who was tyrannizing our nature, and on Thine arising hast Thou filled everything with joy. Wherefore we cry out unto Thee: O Lord, risen from the dead, glory to Thee.

O Christ the Saviour, do Thou through Thy cross lead us unto Thy truth and deliver us from the snares of the enemy; Thou—Risen from the dead, do raise us up fallen on account of the sin, stretching Thine arm, O Lord—Lover of men, through the prayers of Thy saints.

Without departing from Thy Father's bosom, Thou—the Only-begotten Word of God through compassion camest down to the earth, becoming immutably a man, and sufferedst the cross and death in flesh, being impassible in divinity; and on rising again from the dead, Thou hadst granted immortality unto the race of men, as the only All-powerful.

Other, Eastern Sticheras.

Thou sufferedst death in flesh, O Saviour, interceding for our immortality, and Thou didst dwell in the grave, that Thou mayest deliver us from the hades, raising us up together with Thee, for as man didst Thou suffer, but hast risen as God.

Wherefore we cry out: O Lord—Giver of life, glory to Thee, the only Lover of man.

Stones were falling out, O Saviour, when Thy cross was set up on Golgotha, the doorkeepers of the hades were terrified when Thou wast laid in the tomb as dead, for, abolishing the stronghold of death, Thou hast granted in Thy resurrection incorruption unto all the dead; O Saviour, Lord, the Life-Giver, glory to Thee.

The women were desirous of seeing Thy resurrection, O Christ the God. Mary Magdalene, having come before others, found the stone rolled off the grave and the angel who sat there and said: Why seek ye the Living One among the dead? He is risen as God, that He may save all things.

Tell, O ye Jews, where is Jesus Whom you commanded to be guarded? Where is He Whom you have put in the tomb, the stone of which ye have sealed? Give back the Dead One, ye that have rejected the Living, either give up the Buried or believe in the Risen One, for even if you wished to keep the Lord's rising in silence, the stones will cry out, more particularly the one which was rolled off the grave. Great is Thy mercy, great is the mystery of Thine economy, O our Saviour, glory to Thee.

In the Liturgy with the Beatitudes, Tone 4.

Through tree Adam was driven out of paradise; and through the tree of the cross the malefactor became domiciled in paradise, for one in tasting hath rejected the commandment of his Maker and the other, being co-crucified, hath confessed Thee as God hidden, whilst he cried out: Remember me in Thy Kingdom.

Thou, O Lord, that wast raised on the cross, hast destroyed the power of death and wiped off as God the handwriting against us,—grant, O only Lover of man, the contrition of the malefactor unto us also who faithfully serve Thee, O Christ our God, and cry out unto Thee: Remember us also in Thy Kingdom.

The handwriting against us hast Thou torn up with the lance on the cross, and, being reckoned among the dead, Thou hast bound the tyrant of the place, having delivered all from the bonds of the hades by Thy resurrection, wherewith we are enlightened, O Lord—Lover of man, and do cry out unto Thee: Remember also us in Thy Kingdom.

Having been crucified and having risen, as Powerful, from the grave on the third day and having, O only Immortal, raised Adam the first-fashioned, vouchsafe, O Lord, that I also may turn with all my heart unto contrition, and in warm faith continually call unto Thee: Remember me, O Saviour, in Thy Kingdom.

For our sake, He that is impassible hath become passible man, and having been voluntarily nailed on the cross, He hath raised us together with Him; wherefore we glorify also together with the cross His passion and resurrection by which we were re-established, by which also we become saved, calling up: Remember us also in Thy Kingdom.

Him that hath risen from the dead and captured the power of the hades and, whilst He was seen of the myrrh-bearing women, said unto them: Rejoice,—let us, O faithful, entreat to deliver our souls from corruption, ever crying unto Him with the voice of the wise malefactor: Remember us also in Thy Kingdom.

Glory...of the Trinity:

Let us, O faithful, pray that we all may worthily and with one mind doxologise the Father and the Son and the Holy Spirit—unity of God-head remaining in three hypostases unmixed, simple, undivided and inaccessible, wherewith we are delivered from the fiery torments.

Both now...The Theotokion:

Thy Mother, O Christ, that hath brought Thee forth without seed, and a Virgin indeed that hath remained undefiled, after the birth also, her we bring before Thee for entreaty, O Master multigracious, that Thou mayest grant remission of sins unto those that ever cry out unto Thee: Remember us also in Thy Kingdom.

The Prokeimenon: Tone 4.

How magnificent are Thy works, O Lord; all things hast Thou made in wisdom.

Verse: Bless the Lord, O my soul, O Lord, my God, Thou art become exceedingly exalted. (Psalm 103, 24. 2).

Alleluia: Gird Thee and prosper and reign because of truth and meekness and righteousness.

Verse: Thou hast loved righteousness and hated iniquity. (Psalm 44, 5. 8).

ON SATURDAY, AT THE GREAT VESPERS.

For "O Lord, I have cried" the Sticheras of the resurrection, Tone 5.

By Thy honourable cross, O Christ, Thou hast shamed the devil and by Thy resurrection hast blunted the sting of sin and saved us from the gates of death; we glorify Thee, the Only-begotten One.

He Who granteth resurrection unto the human race, as a sheep to the slaughter was led: the princes of the hades were afraid of Him and lifted up were the gates of lamentations *; for Christ, the King of glory, hath entered, saying unto those in chains: Go forth, and to those in darkness: Come up to light.

O great wonder! The Creator of the invisible, having through His love to men, suffered in the flesh, hath risen immortal. Come, O ye descendants of the nations, let us adore Him, for having been, through His tenderness of heart, delivered from enchantment, we learned to hymn One God in three hypostases.

Other, Eastern Sticheras, the same Tone:

Vespertine worship we offer Thee, the never-fading Light, that in the end of the ages through the flesh as in a mirror hast appeared unto the world and hast descended even into the hades and dispersed the darkness there prevailing, and hast shewn unto the nations the light of the resurrection; O Lord—Giver of light, glory to Thee.

---

* Psalm 23, 7.

We doxologise Christ, the Head of our salvation, for since He hath risen from the dead, the world hath been saved from enchantment; the choir of angels rejoiceth, disappeareth seduction of the demons, the fallen Adam is up again, the devil abolished.

The watchmen were thus instructed by the lawless: Conceal the rising of Christ, and take money, and say that, whilst ye were asleep, the Dead One was stolen from the grave. Who ever saw, who hath heard at any time of a dead being stolen, more especially anointed, yet naked, and with the things appertaining to burial being left behind in the grave? Do not be deceived, O ye Jews, study the prophetic sayings and learn that He is truly the Redeemer of the world and All-powerful.

O Lord, that hast spoiled the hades and trodden death under foot, Thou, our Saviour, that hast enlightened the world by Thy honourable cross, have mercy upon us.

Glory...Both now...The Theotokion:

In the Red Sea a likeness of the unmarried bride was once depicted: there Moses was the divider of the water, here Gabriel did the service of the miracle; then Israel walked across the deep dryshod, and now the Virgin without seed hath brought forth Christ; the sea, after Israel had walked over, remained impassable, the spotless one, after the Emmanuel's birth, remained incorrupt; O Thou that art and ever before wast, that did appear as man, have mercy upon us, O God.

For Versicles the Sticheras of the resurrection, Tone 5.

Thee, the Incarnate Saviour, Christ, that didst not forsake the heavens also, we magnify in voices of songs, for as Lord, Lover of man, Thou hast suffered the cross and death, and having overthrown the gates of the hades, rose again on the third day, saving our souls.

Other Sticheras, in alphabetical order:

Whilst Thy side was pierced, Thou hast, O Life-giver, poured out streams of forgiveness, of life and salvation unto all, and in the flesh Thou hast suffered death, granting immortality unto us, and by Thy dwelling in the grave Thou hast freed us, gloriously having raised us with Thee as God. Wherefore we cry aloud: O Lord, Lover of man, glory to Thee.

Wonderful is Thy crucifixion and the descent into the hades, O Lover of man, for having captured it and having gloriously as God raised together with Thee the captives of old, Thou openedst the paradise and madest them worthy thereof; wherefore do also grant unto us that glorify Thy rising on the third day, the propitiation of our sins, making us worthy to be the dwellers of the paradise, as the only Tender-hearted One.

Do Thou that, for our sake, hast in flesh endured the passion and risen from the dead on the third day, cure the passions of our flesh and raise us up from grievous transgressions, O Lover of man, and save us.

Glory...Both now...the Theotokion.

Both temple and gate, palace and throne of the King, art thou, O all-sacred Virgin, through whom Christ the Lord my Redeemer, hath appeared unto those that were sleeping in darkness, He being the Sun of righteousness and desiring to enlighten those whom He had fashioned with His hand after His own image; wherefore, O all-hymned one, since thou possessest the boldness of a mother, do unceasingly pray to Him that our souls may be saved.

The Troparion, Tone 5.

The Word co-unoriginate with the Father and the Spirit, that was born of the Virgin for our salvation, let us, O faithful, hymn and adore; for He was pleased to ascend the cross in flesh and to endure death, and to raise the dead by His glorious resurrection.

The Theotokion:

Hail, O gate of the Lord impassable, hail, O wall and shelter of those that flee unto thee, hail, thou untroubled haven and pure from marital intercourse, that didst bring forth in flesh thy Maker and God; cease not to intercede for those that hymn and adore Whom thou broughtest forth.

At the Matins, after the 1*st Stichologia, the Cathismata of the resurrection, Tone* 5.

Let us eulogize the Lord's cross, let us honour the holy burial with hymns and His resurrection most highly glorify, for He hath as God raised together with Him the dead from their graves, having abolished the dominion of death and the might of the devil, and hath shone forth as light unto those in the hades.

O Lord, Thou wast called dead Who didst destroy death, Thou wast laid in a tomb Who didst empty the tombs; whilst soldiers guarded Thy grave above, Thou didst raise up from below those that were dead for ages; O All-powerful and Incomprehensible Lord, glory to Thee.

Glory...Both now...the Theotokion :

Hail, O holy mount and divine passage; hail, O living and inconsumable bush; hail, O sole bridge for the world toward God which conducteth the dead unto everlasting life; hail, O incorrupt Maiden that without man broughtest forth the salvation of our souls.

After the 2*nd Stichologia, the Cathismata of the resurrection, Tone* 5.

O Lord, after Thy resurrection on the third day and after the worship of the apostles, Peter cried aloud unto Thee: The women had boldness and I was afraid; the malefactor confessed Thee God, and I denied Thee. Wilt Thou then no longer call me a disciple? or wilt Thou again appoint me a fisher of the deep? But receive me repentant, O God, and save me.

O Lord, in the midst of the condemned have the lawless nailed Thee and with a spear they have pierced Thy side, O Merciful; Thou hast submitted to the burial Who destroyedst the gates of the hades, and hast risen on the third day. The women have run up to see Thee, and have announced Thine awaking; O most exalted Saviour, Whom the angels hymn, O blessed Lord, glory to Thee.

Glory...Both now...the Theotokion :

O bride that hast known no man, O God's parent that didst turn the sorrow of Eve into joy! We, the faithful, hymn and adore thee, for thou hast led us up from the ancient curse; do now also unceasingly entreat, O all-hymned, all-holy one, that we may be saved.

The Hypakoe, Tone 5 :

Amazed in their mind at the sight of the angel and in their souls enlightened by the divine awaking, the myrrh-bearing women announced to the apostles: Proclaim among the nations the resurrection of the Lord, Who aideth with wonders and granteth unto us great mercy.

The Graduals, Tone 5. *Antiphon* 1.

In mine affliction, as David I sing to Thee, O my Saviour: Deliver my soul from a deceitful tongue.*

Unto those in the desert life is happiness under the wings of divine love.† [*Glory.*

By the Holy Spirit are governed all things both visible and invisible, for He is Autocrat, truly One of the Trinity.

Both now...the same. Antiphon 2.

To the mountains, O my soul, let us be lifted up, go thither whence the help cometh.‡

Thy right hand§, O Christ, may touch me also and preserve from every under-hand dealing. [*Glory.*

Unto the Holy Spirit let us in divine hymns sing: Thou art God, life, solicitude, light, mind; Thou art goodness, Thou reignest unto the ages.

Both now...the same. Antiphon 3.

Being filled with much joy at the words which they said unto me: To the courts of the Lord let us go up, I send up my prayers.||

---

* Psalm 119, 1. 2. † Psalm 119, 5. 6. ‡ Psalm 120, 1.
§ Psalm 120, 5. || Psalm 121, 1.

In the house of David fearful things are accomplished,* for the fire there consumeth every shameful mind. [*Glory.*

Unto the Holy Spirit appertaineth the dignity of the origin of life, since from Him every creature is animated, just as from the Father together with the Son also.

Both now...The Prokeimenon, Tone 5.

Arise, O Lord my God, let Thy hand be lifted up, for Thou dost reign for ever. *Verse.* I will confess unto Thee, O Lord, with my whole heart (Psalm 9, 33. 2.)

The Canon of the resurrection, Tone 5, *Ode* 1. *The Heirmos :*

Both horse and horseman hath Christ overthrown into the Red Sea, destroying the hosts with His exalted arm, but He saved Israel, who sang the hymn of victory.

The thorn-bearing mob of the Hebrews that hath not preserved a motherly affection for Thee, O Benefactor, did crown Thee, O Christ—the Origin of a race, that hast remitted the chastening of thorns.

Thou hast raised me fallen into the pit, by coming down to me, O Life-giver, Sinless One, and having endured my malodorous corruption, without being infected thereby, Thou hast, O Christ, communicated to me the sweet-smelling myrrh of the divine substance. [*The Theotokion.*

The curse is remitted, the sorrow is over, for the blessed one and full of grace hath emitted unto the faithful gladness, bringing forth as a flower—Christ—blessing unto all the ends.

Another Canon of the cross and resurrection. Tone 5.

Ode 1. *The Heirmos ;* Unto the Saviour God...

Unto Him that was voluntarily nailed in His body to the cross and hath freed from the ancient condemnation the one fallen through the tree,—unto Him alone let us sing, for He is glorified.

Unto Christ, the Dead One, that rose up from the grave and the fallen one hath raised together with Himself and adorned

---

* Psalm 121, 5.

with co-sitting with the Father, unto Him alone let us sing, for He is glorified. [*The Theotokion.*

O all-purest Mother of God, do unceasingly entreat the God that was incarnate of thee, and hath not left the bosom of the Begetter, to save from every calamity those fashioned by Him.

Another Canon of the all-holy Theotokos, Tone the same. *Ode* 1.
The Heirmos: Both horse and horseman hath Christ overthrown into the Red Sea...

Do move Christ—the Light that dwelled in thee, O all-purest, and illumined the world with the rays of divinity, that He may enlighten all those hymning thee, O Mother-Virgin.

As one adorned with the beauty of the virtues, thou hast, O full of grace, received through the overshadowing of the Spirit beneficent magnificence of Him Who adorneth everything, O all-purest.

Thee of old typifying, the bush on the Sinai was not scorched, O Virgin, from contact with the fire, for as Virgin hast thou brought forth and Virgin yet didst above understanding remain, O Mother-Virgin.

The Catabasis: I will open my mouth...

Ode 3. *The Heirmos:*

Thou that hast set up the earth upon nothing by Thy command and suspended it freely hanging, do Thou, O Christ, stablish Thy Church on the immovable rock of Thy commandments, O only Good One and Lover of man.

It was gall that those, who from a stone drank honey, have brought unto Thee, O Christ, Who did wonders in the wilderness; and vinegar as a thank-offering for manna have rendered Thee the ungrateful youths of Israel.

Those that of old were covered with a light-bearing cloud, have laid in the tomb the Life, Christ, but, having risen by His own power, He granted unto all the faithful the light of the Spirit that mysteriously shadoweth forth from above.

The Theotokion:

Thou, O Mother of God, hast, without knowing a man, and

without mother's labour, born Him Who shone forth from the incorrupt Father; wherefore, as Theotokos, since thou hast given birth to the Incarnate Word, we orthodoxly proclaim thee.

Another, the Heirmos: By the power of Thy cross, O Christ...

Arisen from the tomb art thou, O Christ, Who hast delivered from the corruption of death those that hymn, O Life-giver, Thy voluntary crucifixion.

To anoint Thy body, O Christ, the myrrh-bearing women were hurrying, but, having found it not, they returned hymning Thine arising.

The Theotokion:

Do unceasingly supplicate, O pure one, the One Incarnate from thy side, that may be delivered from the snares of the devil those hymning thee as incorrupt Virgin.

Another, the Heirmos: Thou that hast set up the earth upon nothing...

As the ladder by which the Highest came down to us to restore the corrupted nature,—thou, O pure one, wast now clearly seen of all, for through thee the Most Kind One was pleased to hold converse with the world.

The mystery, O Virgin, that was predestined of old and before the ages foreseen of God Who knowest all, having now at last found its termination in thy bosom, O all-purest, made its appearance.

Absolved was the condemnation of the ancient curse through thy mediation, O all-purest Virgin; for the Lord hath, in His exceeding goodness, made the blessing to flow unto all, having come out of thee, the only glory of men.

Ode 4. The Heirmos:

Thine, O Christ, divine emptying having perspicaciously penetrated, Habbakuk in his terror cried out unto Thee: For the salvation of Thy people, to save Thine anointed art Thou come.

The bitterest waters of the Merra, typifying as in a figure Thine undefiled cross, which doth slay the sinful eating, hast Thou, O Good One, sweetened with a tree.

Cross for the tree of knowledge and gall for sweet food hast Thou, O my Saviour, received, and for the destruction of death Thou sheddedst Thy divine blood. [*The Theotokion.*]

Without contact hast thou uncorruptedly conceived in thy belly and without labour brought forth, and having given birth to God in the flesh, thou didst remain Virgin after the birth also.

Another, The Heirmos: Having heard of the power of the cross...

When the cross was fixed in the ground on Golgotha, broken up were the door posts and eternal gate-keepers and they did cry out: Glory to Thy power, O Lord.

When the Saviour came down as dead unto those in bonds, there arose together with Him those that were dead for ages and they cried out: Glory to Thy power, O Lord. [*The Theotokion.*]

The Virgin gave birth and yet did not go through the experience of a mother; but Mother she is and hath remained Virgin, hymning her we call out: Hail, O Theotokos.

Another, the Heirmos: Thine, O Christ, divine....

With my heart and mind, with my soul and mouth do I most devoutly confess thee, O pure one, as Theotokos, since I enjoy the fruit of salvation and am being saved by thine, O Virgin, intercessions.

He Who hath made all from non-existing things, hath been pleased as Benefactor to be fashioned out of thee, O pure one, for the salvation of those that in faith and with love hymn thee, O all-spotless one.

Thy birth, O all-spotless one, is being hymned by the supermundane choirs rejoicing at the salvation and considering thee as the true Theotokos, O Virgin unpolluted.

Isaiah did name thee a staff from which hath sprang forth unto us a beautiful flower—Christ the God, for the salvation of those that in faith and with love have recourse unto thy shelter.

Ode 5. *The Heirmos* :

Unto Thee that arrayest Thyself with light as with a garment, do I watch, and to Thee I call : Enlighten, O Christ, my darkened soul, as the only Compassionate One.

He Who is the God of glory, shamefully, but voluntarily, hangeth in an inglorious form on the tree, ineffably acquiring for me the divine glory.

Thou hast, O Christ, clothed me with incorruption, having uncorruptedly tasted in the flesh of the corruption of death and shone forth from the tomb on the third day. [*The Theotokion.*]

Having without seed born unto us Christ—the Truth and Deliverance—thou, O Theotokos, hast made free from the curse the nature of our ancestor.

Another, The Heirmos : Watching early we cry out unto Thee....

Thy hands hast Thou, our Saviour, stretched upon the tree, calling all unto Thyself, as Lover of man.

The hades hast Thou spoiled, O my Saviour, at Thy burial and at Thy resurrection hast Thou filled up everything with joy.

Thou, O Life-giver, didst rise from the tomb on the third day and hast made to flow unto all imperishable immortality.

The Theotokion :

As Virgin after thy birth, we hymn thee, O Theotokos, for thou hast brought forth in flesh unto the world God the Word.

Another, the Heirmos : Unto Thee that arrayest Thyself with light...

All prophets have clearly announced thee beforehand, O chaste Theotokos, as one that had to become the Mother of God, for thou alone, O pure one, wast found to be perfectly spotless.

An illuminated cloud of the living water that rained down the shower of incorruptibility—even Christ—unto us, the despairing, we acknowledge thee, O chaste one.

Being the nearest unto thee, the God that tabernacled in thee as the only Compassionate One, hath purely loved thee, the beautiful and spotless one, and sealed with the virginity.

Ode 6. *The Heirmos:*

Do tranquillize, O Master, Christ, the sea of passions infuriated by the soul-destructive tempest and bring me out of corruption, as Compassionate One.

Into corruption hath glided our progenitor, O Master, Christ, having partaken of the forbidden food, and unto life was brought up again by Thy passion.

Being the Life, Thou, O Master, Christ, hast come down to the hades and having been corruption unto the seducer, by means of corruption hast Thou caused the resurrection to flow.

[*The Theotokion:*

The Virgin gave birth and having brought forth and carried in her arms Him Who upholdeth everything, she remained pure, as truly Virgin-Mother.

Another, the Heirmos: An abyss hath encompassed me...

Palms of Thy hands hast Thou, O Christ our God, stretched out, gathering Thy peoples far away dispersed into companies by Thy life-bearing cross, as Lover of man.

Death hast Thou made captive and gates of the hades shattered, and Adam having been freed from the chains, cried out unto Thee: Thy right hand hath saved me, O Lord.

[*The Theotokion:*

As bush unconsumed and mountain, as living ladder and gate of heaven we appropriately glorify thee, illustrious Mary, the glory of the orthodox.

Another, the Heirmos: Do tranquillize, O Master, Christ, the sea...

He that is the cause of everything and hath granted life unto all, whilst being incarnate like unto us had thee as a cause, O all-spotless Mother of God.

We know thee, O all-spotless one, as a soul-nourishing source from which spring cures unto those who in faith have recourse underneath thine illustrious shelter, O Sovereign Lady.

Being the cause of salvation, Life-giver hast thou brought forth unto us Who granteth eternal deliverance unto those that proclaim thee true Theotokos.

The Contakion. Tone 5. Similar to: The word Co-unoriginate...

Into the hades, O my Saviour, didst Thou descend, and having shattered the gates as All-powerful, Thou hast, as Creator, raised the dead conjointly with Thee, and hast destroyed the sting of death, Adam also hath been delivered from the curse, O Thou Lover of man, wherefore we all call out: O Lord, save us. [*The Oikos:*

Hearing the sayings of the angel, the women left off their lamentations, became joyful and tremulous, for they saw terrible things, and—behold—Christ hath approached them saying: Hail! have courage, I obtained victory over the world, and set free those in bonds; hasten therefore to the disciples, announcing unto them that I shall meet you in the city of Gallilee for preaching. Wherefore we all call unto Thee: Save us, O Lord.

Ode 7. The Heirmos:

The most exalted Lord of the fathers hath subdued the flame and bedewed the youths who were harmoniously singing: O God, blessed art Thou.

Having clothed Thyself with flesh, Thou hast with Thy divine might, as he with the angling-rod of flattery, hurled down the serpent, leading up those that cry aloud: O God, blessed art Thou.

He who hath brought together into one substance the incompatible parts of the earth is in flesh confined in the grave, although boundless, unto Whom we all sing: O God, blessed art Thou. [*The Theotokion:*

One single hypostasis in two natures didst thou, O all-spotless one, bring forth—God Incarnate, unto Whom we all sing: O God, blessed art Thou.

Another, the Heirmos: In a fiery furnace the melodists...

Thou Who by the tree of the cross hast undone the enchantment of the idols, blessed art Thou, O God of our fathers.

Thou Who hast risen from the dead and brought up together with Thee those in the hades, blessed art Thou, O God of our fathers.

Thou, O Christ, Who by Thy death hast destroyed the dominion of death, blessed art Thou, O God of our fathers.

[*The Theotokion:*

Thou Who art born of the Virgin and hast manifested her as Theotokos, blessed art Thou, O God of our fathers.

Another, the Heirmos: The most exalted Lord of the fathers...

The Uncircumscribed, whilst remaining unchanged, hath, as Compassionate One, united Himself hypostatically unto the flesh in thee, O all-holy one,—the only Blessed God of our fathers.

A bride all spotless we harmoniously glorify in thee, O Theotokos, Sovereign-Lady, and a throne of thy Creator, unto Whom we all sing: O God, blessed art Thou.

Thou, O Virgin, purified by the Spirit, wast become the Mother of the King of all Who hath fashioned thee, and unto Whom we all sing: O God, blessed art Thou.

The Lord hath saved me, having clothed Himself with the raiment of flesh out of thee, O all-spotless Mother of God; unto Him we all sing: O God, blessed art Thou.

Ode 8. *The Heirmos:*

Unto Thee, the Maker of all things, the youths in the furnace, having formed an exquisite choir, sung: Hymn the Lord, all ye the works, and exalt Him unto all the ages.

Thou hast prayed respecting the voluntary cup of Thy saving passion as if it were involuntary, shewing thereby two desires, for one for each of the two natures dost Thou, O Christ, possess unto the ages.

With Thine all-accomplishing descension, O Christ, the derided hades vomited all those that of old were slain through deceit and are exalting Thee unto all the ages. [*The Theotokion:*

Thee that, above all understanding, hast theandrically by the Word brought forth the Lord and remaineth Virgin we, all the works, bless thee, O Virgin, and exalt unto all the ages.

Another, the Heirmos: From the Father before ages...

Him that did His palms voluntarily stretch on the cross and the chains of death hath burst—even Christ the God sing, O ye priests, and ye people—exalt unto all the ages.

Him that as a Bridegroom did shine forth from the grave and unto the myrrh-bearing women hath appeared and announced to them gladness—even Christ the God sing, O ye priests and ye people—exalt unto all the ages. [*The Theotokion :*

Higher than the Cherubim hast thou, O pure Theotokos, appeared having borne in thy belly Him that is being carried on those ; Him with the Incorporeal let us men bless unto all the ages.

Another, the Heirmos : Unto Thee, the Maker of all things...

The sorrow of our first parents hath now ceased, since thou, O Mother of God, hast received gladness. Wherefore we continually hymn thee, O Virgin, and exalt unto all the ages.

With us doth sing the company of the Incorporeal thine, O Virgin, impenetrable bringing forth, having lovingly formed one choir, and exalteth it unto the ages.

A limpid current of immortality hath sprung out of thee, O Maiden, even the Lord of all that cleanseth the filth of all those who in faith hymn thee and exalt unto all the ages.

As a truly divine and light-bearing throne and tablet of grace do we confess thee, O Virgin, since thou hast received the Word of the Father, Whom we exalt unto all the ages.

Ode 9. The Heirmos ;

Isaiah, exult ! The Virgin had in the belly and bare a Son, Emmanuel, both God and man, Orient is His name ; Him magnifying, we glorify the Virgin.

Fallen man hast Thou, O Master Christ, taken up, having united Thyself in the virginal womb unto him entirely, but not partaken of any sin ; Thou hast freed the whole of him from corruption by Thine undefiled passion.

With the emptying of the divine blood from Thine, O Master-Christ, undefiled and life-giving side, sacrifice unto idols hath ceased and all the earth doth bring unto Thee the sacrifice of praise. [*The Theotokion :*

Neither bodiless God nor again a simple man hath the pure and honoured Maiden produced, but a perfect man and verily perfect

God; Him together with the Father and the Spirit do we magnify.

Another, the Heirmos: Thee as above understanding...

Thee Who hast endured sufferings on the cross, and the power of the hades with Thy death hast destroyed, we, the faithful, orthodoxly magnify.

Thee Who hast on the third day from the grave arisen, and the hades despoiled and the world enlightened, we, the faithful, single-mindedly magnify. [*The Theotokion.*

Hail, O Theotokos, Mother of Christ the God! Whom thou barest do entreat to grant the remission of sins unto us that in faith hymn thee.

Another, the Heirmos: Isaiah, exult...

Out of thy pure blood hath supernaturally grown unto the Fashioner of all, the Only-begotten Son of the Begetter, the intellectual and living flesh, not from a man and without seed, O Theotokos-Ever-virgin.

An escape from the unrestrainable stream of death hast thou provided, having, truly above understanding, brought forth in the flesh the Life Eternal, the Which having been merely touched by the bitter mouth of the hades the latter was abolished, O all-holy Mother-Virgin.

Sitting on the throne as Lord, thy Son thee glittering with golden fringes * of divine virtues hath placed on His right hand, assuring honour of mother unto thee, O all spotless one.

Above understanding is thy birth, O Mother of God, for conception with thee was without a man and delivery virginal, since it is God that was born: Him magnifying we glorify thee, O Virgin.

With the Lauds the Sticheras of the resurrection, Tone 5:

O Lord, whilst the grave was sealed of the lawless, Thou hast come out of the tomb just as Thou wast born of the Theotokos:

---

* Psalm 44, 10. 14.

Thy bodiless angels did not understand how Thou becamest incarnate, and the soldiers watching over Thee did not perceive when Thou hast risen again. Both impressed themselves on those inquiring and appeared as marvels unto those that in faith adore the mystery; do grant unto us, who hymn it, joy and great mercy.

O Lord, the eternal door-posts having shattered and the chains broken, out of the tomb hast Thou arisen, leaving Thy funereal belongings in testimony of Thy true burial of three days, and camest to meet in Galilee, whilst being watched in the grotto. Great is Thy mercy, O Incomprehensible Saviour, have mercy on us and save us.

O Lord, the women run unto the tomb to see Thee, O Christ, Who hast suffered for our sake, and having come found there an angel sitting on a stone rolled off from fright, and he cried out unto them saying: Risen is the Lord, tell unto the disciples, that He hath risen from the dead, saving our souls.

O Lord, just as Thou didst come out from sealed grave, so also whilst the door remained closed enteredst Thou unto Thy disciples, showing them Thy bodily suffering which Thou hast endured, O Long-suffering Saviour; as of the seed of David, Thou hast endured the sores, and as the Son of God, hast delivered the world. Great is Thy mercy, O Incomprehensible Saviour, have mercy on us and save us.

Other, Eastern Stricheras:

O Lord, the King of the ages and Maker of all things, Who for our sake hast in flesh endured crucifixion and burial that Thou mayest free us all from the hades; Thou art our God, beside Thee we know none other.

O Lord, Thy most conspicuous wonders—who can confess? or who shall proclaim Thy terrible mysteries? for having become incarnate, as Thyself willedst, Thou hast manifested the predominancy of Thy power; thus upon Thy cross hast Thou opened paradise unto the malefactor and at Thy burial the door-posts of the hades shattered and with Thy resurrection enriched everything. O Lord Compassionate, glory to Thee.

The myrrh-bearing women, having very early reached Thy grave, were searching for Thee to anoint with spices the immortal Word and God; and, having heard the words of the angel, were joyously returning to openly announce unto the apostles that Thou hast arisen, O Life of all, and vouchsafed unto the world expiation and great mercy.

The guardians of the God-containing grave said unto the Jews: Woe unto your sophistical counsel! In attempting to watch over the Uncircumscribable One, in vain have ye laboured; desiring to conceal the resurrection of the Crucified One, ye have clearly manifested it. Woe unto your sophistical assembly! Why do ye again counsel us to conceal that which does not admit of hiding? Ye had rather hear from us and desire to believe the truth of what hath taken place: A lightning-bearing angel coming down from heaven, hath rolled off the stone, whereat the deadly fear hath taken hold of us, and raising his voice unto the strong minded myrrh-bearing women, thus spake unto them: Do not ye see the mortification of the guardians, and the loosening of the seals and of the hades the emptying? Why search ye for Him Who hath abolished the triumph of the hades and destroyed the sting of death as a Dead One? Swiftly running do announce unto the apostles the glad tidings of the resurrection, fearlessly calling out: Risen indeed is the Lord, having a great mercy.

At the Liturgy, with the Beatitudes, Tone 5:

The malefactor on the cross believing Thee, O Christ, to be God, confessed Thee with open heart, crying out: Remember me, O Lord, in Thy Kingdom.

Him that on the tree of the cross hath caused life to flourish unto our race and dried up the curse that was from the tree, let us harmoniously hymn as Saviour and Creator.

With Thy death, O Christ, Thou hast destroyed the power of death and raised up together with Thee those who died ages before and are hymning Thee, the True God and our Saviour.

Unto Thy tomb, O Christ, being come, the honourable women

searched for Thee, O Life-giver, to anoint Thee, and an angel appeared unto them crying out: Risen is the Lord.

Whilst Thou, O Christ, wast crucified between two condemned malefactors, one of them, who blasphemed Thee, was rightfully condemned, and the other, having confessed Thee, entered paradise.

Unto the assembly of the apostles being come, the honourable women cried aloud: Christ is risen; as Master and Creator let us adore Him. [*Glory...of the Trinity.*

Trinity indivisible, Unity all-creating and omnipotent, the Father, the Son and the Holy Spririt, Thee we hymn as True God and our Saviour. [*Both now...The Theotokion.*

Hail—the living temple of God and the gate impassable! Hail—the unconsumable and fire-like throne! Hail—the Mother of the Emmanuel, of Christ our God.

The Prokeimenon, Tone 5:

Thou, O Lord, shalt keep us and preserve us from this generation forth and for ever.

The Verse: Save me, O Lord, for there is not one godly man left. (Psalm 11, 8. 2).

Alleluia: Thy mercies, O Lord, I shall hymn for ever, from generation to generation shall I proclaim Thy truth with my mouth.

The Verse: For Thou hast said: Mercy shall be set up for ever: Thy truth shall be established in the heavens. (Psalm 88, 2. 3).

ON SATURDAY, AT THE GREAT VESPERS.

For " O Lord, I have cried" the Sticheras of the resurrection, Tone 6.

Possessing victory over the hades, Thou, O Christ, didst ascend the cross that Thou mightest, together with Thyself Who art free among the dead, raise those that sat in the shades of death; O All-powerful Saviour, Who makest life to spring from Thy light, have mercy upon us.

To-day Christ, having trampled upon death, hath arisen, as He had said, and hath given joy unto the world, that we all may cry in a hymn, thus saying: Thou art the Fountain of life, the Light Inaccessible, have mercy upon us, O All-powerful Saviour.

From Thee, O Lord, Who art everywhere present, whither shall we sinners flee? To heaven? But Thou Thyself dwellest there. To the hades? But Thou hast there trampled upon death. Into the depths of the sea? But even therein is Thy hand, O Master.* Unto Thee we fly for refuge and falling down before Thee we pray: Thou that didst rise from the dead, have mercy upon us.

Other, Eastern Sticheras, Tone the same.

In Thy cross, O Christ, do we glory, and Thy resurrection we hymn and glorify; for Thou art our God, besides Thee we know none other.

Ever blessing the Lord, we hymn His resurrection; for, having endured crucifixion, death by death hath He overthrown.

Glory to Thy might, O Lord, since Thou hast crushed him that had the dominion of death, and hast renewed us by Thy cross, granting unto us life and incorruption.

Thy burial, O Lord, hath utterly destroyed the bonds of the hades, and Thy resurrection from the dead hath enlightened the world; glory to Thee, O Lord.

[*Glory...Both now...the Theotokion:*

---

* Psalm 138, 7-12.

Who would not bless thee, O all-holy Virgin? Who would not hymn thy most spotless child-birth? For He that for ever shone from the Father, even the Only-begotten Son, came forth from thee, O pure one, having become unspeakably incarnate, He that is by nature God became for us by nature man also, not that He was divided into two persons, but that He is known in two unmingled natures. Him, O pure and most blessed one, beseech to have mercy on our souls.

For Versicles the Sticheras, Tone 6.

Thy resurrection, O Christ the Saviour, angels sing in heavens; vouchsafe also unto us upon earth with pure heart Thee to glorify.

In the alphabetical order:

Having shattered the gates of brass and demolished the door-posts of the hades, Thou hast as God All-powerful raised again the fallen race of men, wherefore we also with one accord cry: Thou that art risen from the dead, O Lord, glory to Thee.

Desiring to re-establish our old estate, Christ was nailed to the cross and placed in the grave; and seeking Him with tears the myrrh-bearing women lamentingly spake: Woe unto us, O Saviour of all! How didst Thou deign to dwell within a grave? and if Thou so willedst, how wast Thou stolen? how wast Thou misplaced? and what spot is it that hath concealed Thy quickening body? But, O Master, as Thou hast promised, do appear unto us and assuage our wailing tears. And, whilst they wept, an angel cried unto them: Cease from your lamentations and say to the apostles that the Lord is risen, granting unto the world propitiation and great mercy.

Having been crucified as Thou didst will, and at Thy burial having despoiled death, Thou hast arisen on the third day as God in glory, bestowing upon the world life unending and great mercy. [*Glory...Both now...the Theotokion*:

My Maker and Redeemer, Christ the Lord, having come forth from thy womb, O all pure one, indued with my flesh, hath delivered Adam from the ancient curse. Wherefore unto thee, O all-pure one, as unto truly both Mother of God and Virgin, we do unceasingly cry, as the angel called: "Hail,"—Hail, O Sovereign-Lady, our intercession and protection and salvation of our souls.

The Troparion of the resurrection, Tone 6.

The angelic hosts were upon Thy tomb-stone, the watch became as dead, and Mary stood at the grave, seeking Thine all-pure body. Thou hast despoiled the hades without being ensnared by it; Thou didst meet the Virgin, granting life. Thou that hast risen from the dead, O Lord, glory to Thee.

[*Glory...Both now...the Theotokion:*

Thou that didst call Thy Mother blessed, camest of Thine own free will to the passion, shining on the cross, seeking to recall Adam, saying to the angels: Rejoice with Me, for the drachma that was lost is found.* Thou that hast ordered all things in wisdom, our God, glory to Thee.

On Sunday, at the Matins, after the 1*st Stichologia, the Cathismata of the resurrection, Tone* 6.

Whilst the grave was open and the hades lamenting, Mary cried to the hidden apostles: Come forth, ye workers of the vineyard, preach the word of the resurrection: Risen is the Lord, granting to the world great mercy.

O Lord, at Thy grave stood Mary Magdalene and, taking Thee for a gardener, with loud lamentations thus spake unto Thee: Where hast Thou concealed the Eternal Life? Wherein hast Thou placed Him that sitteth on a cherubic throne? for those who guarded Him became as dead from fear. Either give me back my Lord, or call out with me: Thou that wast among the dead and hast raised the dead,—glory to Thee.

[*Glory...Both now...the Theotokion:*

Gideon doth pre-narrate thy conception and David doth relate thy bringing forth, O Theotokos; for the Word came down into thy womb as the dew upon the fleece,† and without seed hast

---

* Luke 15, 9. † Judges, 6, 37.

thou, O holy land, sprouted forth the salvation of the world, even Christ our God, thou that art full of grace.

After the 2nd Stichologia the Cathismata of the resurrection, Tone 6:

The life was lying in the grave and a seal remained over the stone; as a sleeping King the soldiers guarded Christ, and yet, His enemies invisibly overthrowing, the Lord hath risen.

Jonah doth pre-narrate Thy grave and Simeon doth relate Thy divine awaking, O Lord Immortal, for as a Dead One into the grave didst Thou descend that hast destroyed the gates of the hades, and rose again, without corruption, as Master for the salvation of the world, O Christ, our God, that hath enlightened those sitting in darkness.

[*Glory...Both now...the Theotokion:*

O Theotokos-Virgin! beseech thy Son Who of His free-will was nailed to the cross and arose from the dead, even Christ our God, that our souls may be saved.

After "the Blameless" the Hypakoe, Tone 6:

Having by Thine, O Christ, voluntary and life-giving death shattered the gates of the hades as God, Thou hast opened unto us the ancient paradise, and, having risen from the dead, Thou hast delivered our life from corruption.

Thereupon the Graduals, Tone 6. *Antiphon* 1:

Unto the heaven do I lift up mine eyes, even unto Thee, O Word;* have compassion upon me that I may live to Thee.

Have mercy upon us utterly despised,† making us again Thy serviceable vessels, O Word. [*Glory.*

Unto the Holy Spirit appertaineth an all-saving cause; on whomsoever He worthily breatheth quickly doth He extricate such from things of earth, He wingeth them, maketh them grow, settleth on high.

---

* Psalm 122, 1. † Psalm, 122, 3.

Both now...the same. Antiphon 2.

If the Lord had not been with us, none of us could have withstood the attacks of the enemy*; for the vanquishing are thereby exalted.

Let not my soul be caught as a bird in their teeth, O Word†; woe unto me! how can I escape from the enemy, being a lover of sin? [*Glory...*

Of the Holy Spirit cometh unto all divine inspiration, good-will, understanding, peace and blessing; for He is Co-worker with the Father and the Word.

Both now...the same. Antiphon 3.

They that trust in the Lord‡ are terrible to enemies and wonderful to all men, for they look on high.

Unto iniquity the lot of the righteous does not stretch their hands§, having as helper Thee, O Saviour. [*Glory...*

Unto the Holy Spirit appertaineth the sovereignty over all things; Him worship the hosts above with every breath below.

Both now...the same. The Prokeimenon, Tone 6.

O Lord, stir up Thy strength, and come in order to save us. *The Verse*: Hear, O Thou Shepherd of Israel, Thou that leadest Joseph like a sheep (Psalm 79, 3. 2).

The Canon of the resurrection. Ode 1. *Tone* 6. *The Heirmos*:

Whilst travelling on foot along the depths of the sea as if upon dry land, Israel, seeing Pharaoh, their pursuer, drowned, cried out: Unto God let us sing an ode of victory.

With Thy palms stretched upon the cross, Thou hast, O Good Jesus, filled all things with the Father's good-will; wherefore an ode of victory we all sing unto Thee.

With fear, as a bidden slave, death hath approached Thee—the Sovereign-Lord of life, Who thereby granteth unto us endless life and resurrection. [*The Theotokion:*

---

* Psalm 123, 2. † Psalm 123, 6-7.
‡ Psalm 124, 1. § Psalm 124, 3.

Thy Maker having received, as He Himself willed, when He was, above all understanding, within thy seedless womb becoming incarnate, thou hast appeared, O pure one, truly Sovereign-Lady of all things created.

Another Canon of the cross and resurrection. Ode 1. *The Heirmos:* Him Who of old hath...

Before Pilate's judgment-seat, unlawfully accused, doth voluntarily stand as one condemned the Judge, and of a hand of wickedness is smitten on the face the God before Whom do tremble both the earth and the heavenly things.

Thy divine palms hast Thou, O Saviour, stretched upon Thine unpolluted and life-bearing cross, and Thou hast gathered unto a perfect knowledge of Thee, O Master, the peoples that adore Thine, O Lord, glorious crucifixion. [*The Stavro-theotokion:*

At Thy cross, O Saviour, stood the all-spotless one, shedding fountains of tears, looking at the drops of blood oozing from Thy side and glorifying Thine incomparable compassion, O Christ.

Another Canon of the all-holy Theotokos. The Heirmos: Whilst travelling on foot along...

Through participating of the forbidden fruit of the garden, Eve hath brought on the curse, but this thou, O pure one, hast undone having given birth to Christ—Origin of blessing.

Having given birth to Christ—a Pearl of the divine lightning, do thou, O pure one, disperse the mist of my passions and the confusion of my transgression with the light of thy brightness.

The Hope of the peoples becoming incarnate of thee, the God that hath delivered us through thine intercession, Jacob did contemplate within himself with the eyes of his mind.*

The princes of the tribe of Judah having disappeared, thy Son and God, O all-purest, having come down as a Chieftain, is now truly enthroned over the ends of the earth.

---

* Genesis 49, 10.

The Catabasis : I will open my mouth ...
Ode 3. The Heirmos.

There is none holy as Thou, O Lord my God, that hast, as Good One, exalted the horn of Thy believers, and established us upon the rock of Thy confession.

Seeing God crucified in flesh, the creation was breaking up from fear; but was mightily held together by the sustaining palm of Him Who for our sake was crucified.

Death destroyed by death is lying miserably without breath, for, unable to bear the divine advance of the Life, the strong one dieth and resurrection is bestowed on all. [*The Theotokion :*

The wonder of thy divine child-birth, O pure one, surpasseth every order of nature, for God hast thou supernaturally conceived in thy womb, and having given birth remainest Ever-virgin.

Another, the Heirmos : Beholding Thee Who hast the whole earth suspended....

Having remained three days in the grave, Thou hast raised with Thy life-giving awaking those slain before, and freed from condemnation, they were joyously exultant and called out: Behold, as the redemption art Thou come, O Lord.

Glory to Thine awaking, O our Saviour, for Thou hast delivered us, as All-powerful, from the hades, corruption and death, and melodizing Thee we say: There is none holy as Thou, O Lord, Lover of man. [*The Theotokion :*

Seeing Him that was born of thee pierced with a lance, thou, O most holy all-spotless one, felt pierced through thy heart and in utter amazement saidst: What hath rendered unto Thee, O Child, this most wicked people?

Another, the Heirmos : There is none holy as Thou....

My transient and mortal flesh having out of thine, O all-pure Mother of God, belly ineffably taken and made it incorruptible, the Good One hath for ever united it unto Himself.

Seeing God becoming incarnate of thee, O Virgin, the choirs of angels were amazed, and as Mother of God honour thee in never-ceasing hymns.

The prophet Daniel was frightened when contemplating thee—the intellectual mount from which a stone was cut out without hands * that hath mightily demolished the temples of the demons, O Mother of God.

Neither word of man nor human tongue can worthily praise thee, O Virgin, for of thee, O all-pure one, hath deigned to become incarnate, without seed, Christ the Life-giver.

Ode 4. *The Heirmos.*

Christ is my power, my God and Lord—the venerable church God-beseemingly singeth, thus calling out, with pure mind feasting in the Lord.

The tree hath blossomed with true life, O Christ, for the cross hath been set up and, having been soaked with blood and water from Thine incorruptible side, hath sprouted life unto us.

No longer doth the serpent fraudulently submit to me the deification,† for Christ, the Divine Maker of human nature, hath now opened unto me without any forbidding the path of life. [*The Theotokion:*

Truly unutterable and incomprehensible are the mysteries of thine, O Theotokos, God-worthy child-bearing, both unto those of earth and those of heaven, O Ever-virgin.

Another, the Heirmos: Foreseeing Thy divine emptying on the cross....

Thy honourable cross and nails, O Christ, we venerate, as well as the holy spear with the reed and the crown of thorns by which we were delivered from the corruption of the hades.

The grave hath taken Thee, O Saviour, Who voluntarily for our sake hast died, but could not possibly hold Thee, O Word, for as God hast Thou risen again, saving our race.

[*The Stavro-Theotokion:*

---

* Dan. 2, 34. † Genesis 3, 5.

O God's Mother, Ever-virgin, that hast brought forth unto men Christ the Saviour, from dangers and torments do deliver us that in faith have recourse unto thy divine shelter.

Another, the Heirmos: Christ is my power ..

Thee all-spotless, O purest one, we hymn, having been saved by thee, and proudly singing call out: Blessed art thou, O Ever-virgin, that gave birth to God.

The Light never disappearing, shining through flesh, O Virgin, hast thou brought forth unto those that are in the life's darkness, O all-blessed one, and unto those that hymn thee, O Ever-virgin, hast made gladness to flow.

The grace hath blossomed, the law ceased through thee, O all-holy one; for thou, O pure one, hast given birth to the Lord that granteth us, O Ever-virgin, forgiveness.

Eating in the garden hath brought me to death, but the tree of life that came forth of thee, O purest one, hath raised me again and made me heir of the sweets of paradise.

Ode 5. *The Heirmos:*

With Thy divine light, O Good One, do illumine, I pray Thee, the souls of those who lovingly watch early unto Thee, that they may know Thee, O Word of God, as the true God, recalling them out of the darkness of sin.

Now the cherubim do not stand in my way and the flaming sword, O Master, is turned back, since they saw, O Word of God, Thee, the true God, making for the malefactor the way into paradise.

No longer do I fear returning unto earth, O Master—Christ;* for, in Thy great compassion, Thou hast led me, utterly forgotten one, from earth unto the height of incorruption, through Thy resurrection. [*The Theotokion:*

Save, O good Sovereign-Lady of the world, those that from their soul confess thee as Theotokos; for in thee we possess invincible protection, the true Mother of God.

---

* Genes. 3, 19.

Another, the Heirmos: Of Thy divine manifestation, O Christ...

Tempted in Eden with the fruit of the tree, the progenitor hath slid down into corruption,* having, O Lord, disobeyed Thine, O All-good One, commandment; but him hast Thou led up again unto the beauty through Thy cross, having been, O Saviour, obedient to the Father.

At Thy death, O Good One, the dominion of death hath been done away with, source of life was made to flow unto us and immortality was bestowed; wherefore we adore in faith Thy burial and resurrection, wherewith Thou as God enlightened all the world. [*The Stavro-Theotokion:*

Abiding in heavens, the Lord and Maker of everything did into thine, O all-spotless one, womb ineffably enter, glorifying thee as incomparably higher than the heavens and holier than the incorporeal orders; wherefore we that are now on earth, bless thee.

Another, the Heirmos: With Thy divine light...

Having brightly shined with purity, thou, O all-hymned one, becamest divine abode of the Master, for thou alone didst appear as Mother of God, having carried Him as infant in thine arms.

Full of the intellectual ornaments of thy most beautiful soul, thou wast God's bride, being sealed with the modest virginity and enlightening the world with the brightness of purity.

Let the assembly of the wicked, those that do not proclaim thee openly as pure God's Mother, lament, for thou hast appeared unto us as the gate of divine light scattering the darkness of sins.

Ode 6. *The Heirmos:*

Beholding the sea of life swelling with the storm of temptations, and taking refuge in Thy calm haven, I cry unto Thee: Lead up my life from corruption, O greatly merciful One.

Being crucified, with the nails hast Thou, O Master, annulled the curse that was upon us, and Thy side being pierced with the

* Genes. 3, 19.

lance, whilst Thou hast torn up the handwriting against Adam, Thou hast freed the world.

Adam being deceitfully smitten in the heel was led down to the pit of the hades, but Thou Who art by nature both God and Compassionate, camest down to recall him and, having carried him on Thy shoulder,* hast raised him together with Thyself.

[*The Theotokion:*

O all-holy Sovereign-Lady, who hast brought forth unto men in the Lord the Pilot, do calm of my passions the ever changing and terrible surgings and grant tranquillity unto my heart.

Another, the Heirmos: Jonah was swallowed by the whale, but not retained...

Christ-slayers and prophet-killers was the Hebrew multitude, for just as it was not afraid to kill prophets that of old were the mysterious rays of the truth, so now, carried by envy, it hath slain the Lord also, of Whom those in their time preached; but unto us His being put to death is become life.

Thou wast confined in the tomb but not detained therein, O Saviour, for though willingly Thou hast tasted of death, O Word, yet didst Thou arise as God immortal, having awakened together with Thee the captives in the hades and unto the women having exchanged gladness for the former sorrow.

[*The Theotokion:*

More ignominious and despised than of any man appeared Thy bodily aspect at the time of the passion,† for by nature of the Divinity Thou seemedst unto David as the fairest in beauty; ‡ but the pure one thus spake unto Thee that with the sceptre of Thy Kingdom the strength of the enemies hast destroyed: O my Son and God, rise up from the grave.

Another, the Heirmos: Beholding the sea of life...

The great among the prophets Moses described thee beforehand as ark and table, candlestick and pot,§ in symbols signifying the incarnation of the Most High from thee, O Mother-Virgin.

* Luke 15, 4. 5. † Isaiah, 53, 3. ‡ Psalm 44, 3. § Exod. 40, 3. 4. 5.

Death is slain and corruption—the curse of Adam—abolished in consequence of their attack upon thine Offspring, O Sovereign-Lady, for thou hast given birth to Life that delivereth from corruption those who hymn thee.

The law became impotent and the shadow passed away when, above understanding and comprehension, there appeared unto me the grace of the birth by thee, O greatly hymned Virgin, of the God and Saviour.

The Contakion, Tone 6.

Having with the vivifying hand as Life-giver raised the dead from the dark valleys of misery, Christ the God of all hath granted resurrection to the whole human race, for He is the Saviour of all, the Resurrection and the Life and the God of all.

[*The Oikos :*

Thy cross and burial, O Life-giver, we the faithful hymn and adore, for as God All-powerful Thou, O Immortal One, hast bound the hades and raised together with Thee the dead; Thou as God hast shattered the gates of death and laid low the power of the hades; wherefore we, the earth-born, lovingly glorify Thee Who, as God of all, hast arisen, overthrown the all-destructive dominion of the enemy, raised all those that believed in Thee, and delivered the world both from the serpent's darts and the adversary's wiles.

Ode 7. *The Heirmos :*

Dew-yielding hath an angel made the furnace unto the pious youths, and God's injunction burning the Chaldeans hath inclined the tyrant to cry out: Blessed art Thou, O God of our fathers.

Bewailing Thy passion the sun hath wrapped himself in darkness and upon all the earth, O Master, in the day time, the light grew dim crying out: Blessed art Thou, O God of our fathers.

At Thy descent, O Christ, the lowest depths were surrounded with light, and the forefather, full of joy and exultant, sprung up crying: Blessed art Thou, O God of our fathers.

[*The Theotokion :*

Through thee, O Mother-Virgin, bright light rose up unto all the universe, for thou hast brought forth the Maker of all—God; Him entreat, O all-pure one, to send down upon us, the faithful, great mercy.

Another, the Heirmos: O wonder ineffable...

O strange spectacle! He Who hath delivered Israel from Pharaoh's bondage is crucified by them of His own will and doth loose the bonds of sin; unto Him we in faith sing: O God the Redeemer, blessed art Thou.

The children of the wicked have crucified on the calvary Thee, the Saviour, that hast broken up the gates of brass and the door-posts unto the salvation of us who sing: O God the Redeemer, blessed art Thou.

The Theotokion: Having brought forth the Deliverance of ancient Eve, thou, O pure Virgin, dost free Adam from the curse; wherefore together with angels we hymn thee with thy Son and cry out: O God the Redeemer, blessed art Thou.

Another, the Heirmos: Dew-yielding hath an angel made the furnace....

The furnace did not hurt the three youths, thus prefiguring thy child-birth; for the divine Fire, without burning thee, hath dwelled in thee and taught every one to cry out: Blessed art Thou, O God of our fathers.

The ends call thee blessed, O all-pure Mother, as thou hast prophesied; being enlightened with lustrous beams of thy beauty and grace, they make melody of their cry: Blessed art Thou, O God of our fathers.

Destructive teeth hath plunged into me the most cunning serpent, but these thy Son, O Mother of God, hath broken and unto me gave strength to cry out: Blessed art Thou, O God of our fathers.

Cleanser of nature art only thou, O God's blessed one, for having carried in thine arms God Who sitteth on cherubim's shoulders, thou dost cry out: Blessed art Thou, O God of our fathers.

Ode 8. The Heirmos:

Unto the pious hast Thou made dew out of the flame to flow and the sacrifice of a righteous man didst Thou consume with water, for everything makest Thou, O Christ, just as Thou willest; Thee we exalt unto all the ages.

The Jewish people, the prophet-killers of old, hath envy made now God-slayers that raised Thee on the cross, O Word of God, Whom we exalt unto all the ages.

Heavenly circles didst Thou not leave and, having descended into the hades, Thou hast raised together with Thyself, O Christ, man lying in corruption that exalteth Thee unto all the ages.

The Theotokion: Of Light hast thou conceived Lightgiver, the Word, and having ineffably brought Him forth, wast glorified, for Divine Spirit, O Maiden, hast dwelled in thee. Wherefore we hymn thee unto all the ages. [*The Theotokion:*

Another, the Heirmos: Quake for dread thou, O heaven...

Every ear hath trembled on perceiving how the Most High, of His own will, came down on earth to destroy the domination of the hades by His cross and burial and to awaken all that they may call out: Bless Him, ye youths, hymn Him, ye priests, and ye people, exalt Him unto all the ages.

Tyranny of the hades hath ceased and the dominion thereof consequently became despised, for the God of all having been set up on earth upon the cross, hath laid down his domination; Him bless, O ye youths, ye priests, hymn Him, and ye people, exalt Him unto all the ages.

How ineffable is Thine, O Christ, love to man and how unutterable Thy goodness! For seeing me imprisoned within the hades and perishing, Thou endureth the passion and set me free. Wherefore we bless Thee, the Master of all, and exalt unto all the ages.

Another, the Heirmos: Unto the pious hast Thou made dew out of the flame...

Having with the illumination of the Spirit made thee resplendent as Sovereign in a golden vestment, thy Son hath placed thee, O all-pure one, on His right hand; Him we exalt unto all the ages.

He that with a mere will alone hath set up the world, from thine unpolluted womb taketh flesh desiring to fashion it from above; Him we exalt unto all the ages.

Through the union of the Word with me, a man, thou hast become, O all-pure one, a divine abode, having clearly shined with the lustre of virginity, wherefore we hymn thee unto all the ages.

The candlestick shining with gold hath prefigured thee who ineffably receivedst the Light unapproachable that illumineth everything with His knowledge. Wherefore we hymn thee, O pure one, unto all the ages.

Ode 9. *The Heirmos:*

It is not possible for men to behold God on Whom the angelic orders dare not cast a glance; but through thee, O all-pure one, was seen of men the Incarnate Word; Him magnifying, with heavenly hosts we call thee blessed.

Impassionable didst Thou remain, O Word of God, whilst Thou wast in flesh joined unto passions, and dost free men from passions, having been unto passions a passion, O our Saviour, for Thou alone art Impassible and All-powerful.

Having undergone the corruption of death Thou hast preserved Thy body from decay and Thy vivifying and divine soul, O Master, was not left in the hades,* but arising as from sleep, Thou hast raised us also. [*Of the Trinity:*

God the Father, the Son Co-unoriginate we, all men, with pure lips do glorify and honour the ineffable and most glorious power of the All-holy Spirit; for Thou art alone All-powerful, O Trinity inseparable.

Another, the Heirmos: Bewail me not, O Mother.......

Although into the grave as dead didst Thou descend, O Life-giver, yet hast Thou, O Christ, destroyed the power of the hades, having raised together with Thyself those that were

* Psalm 15, 10.

engulfed therein, and granted, as God, resurrection unto all that with faith and love magnify Thee.

Let the creation be transported with delight and blossoming as a lily, for Christ is risen from the dead as God; let us call out: Death! where is now thy sting? and thy victory, O hades?* He Who hath exalted our horn, as Compassionate One, laid thee to the ground. [*The Stavro-Theotokion:*

Thou bearest, O most pure Sovereign-Lady, Him Who beareth everything, and holdest in thine arms as infant, Him Who delivereth us from the hand of the warring enemy, and beholdest on the tree of the cross being lifted Him Who hath raised us up from the pit of wickedness.

Another, the Heirmos: It is not possible for men to behold God....

A star resplendent with the lustre of divinity hath from Jacob arisen unto those that were held in darkness, for through thee, O all-pure one, Christ the God hath now become incarnate Word; by Him being enlightened, with heavenly hosts we call thee blessed.

Strengthened by thy power and grace, I have composed this ode unto thee from ardent heart; do accept it, O pure Virgin, sending down in return from the imperishable treasures thy multifarious grace, O blessed of God.

Divine loom hast thou manifestly become, upon which the Word hath woven a covering of flesh, having made, O Virgin, God-like my form; and having put this on, He hath saved all those that with pure mind magnify thee.

Upon the dead resurrection hath now been bestowed through thine unspeakable and ineffable child-birth, O all-pure Theotokos, for Life, having put on flesh from thee, shone unto all, and the decay of death hath manifestly destroyed.

With the Lauds the Sticheras of the resurrection, Tone 6.

Thy cross, O Lord, is life and resurrection unto Thy people, and trusting thereon we hymn unto Thee, our Risen God: Have mercy upon us.

* I Corinth. 15, 25; Hos. 13, 14.

Thy burial, O Master, hath opened paradise unto the race of men, and having been delivered from corruption we hymn unto Thee, our Risen God: Have mercy upon us.

With the Father and the Spirit let us hymn Christ, risen from the dead, and unto Him let us cry: Thou art our Life and Resurrection, have mercy upon us.

Risen art Thou on the third day, O Christ, from the grave as it was written, having raised together with Thyself our forefather. Wherefore the race of men both glorifieth Thee, and hymneth Thy resurrection.

Other, Anatolian Sticheras.

O Lord, great and dreadful is the mystery of Thy resurrection, for, as a Bridegroom cometh from the palace, so didst Thou proceed from the grave, overcoming death by death, to deliver Adam. Wherefore angels in heaven exult and men on earth glorify the compassion shewn unto us by Thee, O Lover of man.

O most wicked Jews! Where are the seals and the silver pieces which ye have handed to the watchmen? The Treasure was not stolen, but arose as Powerful, and ye were put to shame who have denied Christ—the Lord of glory, that hath suffered, was buried and arose from the dead; Him let us adore.

The tomb being sealed, how could ye Jews be robbed, since you placed the watch and affixed seals? The King hath passed through whilst the doors were closed. Either produce Him as dead, or worship Him as God, singing with us: Glory, O Lord, to Thy cross and resurrection.

The myrrh-bearing women having, with loud lamentations, reached Thy life-containing tomb and, carrying spices, sought to anoint Thy purest body; and they found a radiant angel sitting on the stone, who was addressing them and saying: Why do ye deplore Him Who hath made life to flow from His side unto the world? Why do ye seek the Immortal One among the dead in the tomb? Rather make haste to announce to His disciples the universal joy of His glorious resurrection. Enlightening also us therewith, grant unto us, O Saviour, expiation and great mercy.

At the Liturgy with the Beatitudes. Tone 6 :

Remember me, O God, my Saviour, when Thou comest in Thy Kingdom, and save me as the sole Lover of man.

Adam having been beguiled by tree, by tree of the cross again hast Thou saved the malefactor also that cried out: Remember me, O Lord, in Thy Kingdom.

Having, O Life-giver, shattered the gates and the door-posts of the hades, Thou hast, O Saviour, raised all that cry out: Glory to Thine awaking.

Remember me, O Thou Who didst spoil death by Thy burial, and hast filled all things with joy by Thy resurrection, as Compassionate One.

The myrrh-bearing women having reached the tomb, heard an angel crying out: Christ is risen that hath enlightened all things.

Let us all harmoniously hymn Christ that was nailed on the tree of the cross and delivered the world from guile.

[*Glory......of the Trinity :*

Let us glorify the Father and the Son and the Holy Spirit, saying: O Holy Trinity, save our souls.

[*Both now......the Theotokion :*

Thou that didst in the end of days ineffably conceive and bring forth thy Maker, save, O Virgin, those that magnify thee.

The Prokeimenon, Tone 6 : Save, O Lord, Thy people and bless Thine inheritance. *The Verse :* Unto Thee, O Lord, will I cry, O my God, do not pass me in silence (*Psalm* 27, 9. 1).

Alleluia : He that dwelleth under the wardship of the Most High, under the shelter of the God of heavens shall abide. *The Verse :* He will say to the Lord: Thou art my protector and my refuge, my God, and in Him shall I trust. (*Psalm* 90, 1. 2).

ON SATURDAY, AT THE GREAT VESPERS.

For "O Lord, I have cried," the Sticheras of the resurrection, Tone 7.

The composition of St. John of Damascus.

Come, let us exult in the Lord Who hath destroyed the dominion of death and enlightened the race of men, crying with the incorporeal: O our Maker and Saviour, glory to Thee.

Cross and burial hast Thou endured, O Christ, for our sake, and by death hast Thou, as God, slain death. Wherefore we adore Thy resurrection on the third day; O Lord, glory to Thee.

Seeing the awaking of the Maker, the apostles were struck with amazement and sung the angelic laud: This is the glory of the Church, this is the wealth of the Kingdom; O Lord that hath suffered for us, glory to Thee.

Other, Eastern Sticheras, the same Tone:

Laid hold of wast Thou, O Christ, by the lawless men, yet unto me Thou art God and I am not ashamed; smitten wast Thou on the cheeks, and I do not deny Thee; on the cross wast Thou nailed, and I do not conceal it; in Thine awaking I glory, for Thy death is my life. O All-powerful, Lord and Lover of man, glory to Thee.

Fulfilling David's prophecy, Christ hath manifested unto the disciples His majesty in Zion,* shewing Himself ever lauded and glorified together with the Father and the Holy Spirit,—at first bodiless as Word and afterwards incarnate and slain for our sake as man, and risen in power, as Lover of man.

Thou didst descend into the hades, as Thou willedst, O Christ; Thou didst overthrow death as God and Master and hast arisen on the third day, having raised from the bonds of the hades and

---

* Psalm 64, 2.

corruption, together with Thyself, those that were crying out and saying: Glory to Thy resurrection, O only Lover of man.

Into the grave wast Thou laid, O Lord, as one that sleepeth, and hast arisen on the third day as One mighty in strength, having raised with Thyself Adam from the corruption of death, as All-powerful. [*Glory... Both now... the Theotokion:*

A Mother above nature art thou become recognized, O Theotokos, yet thou remainedst Virgin above utterance and understanding, and the miracle of Thy child-birth no language can tell. Just as the conception, O pure one, is most glorious, so the manner of birth is incomprehensible, for whenever God willeth, the course of nature is set aside; wherefore acknowledging thee as Mother of God, assiduously do we all implore thee to intercede that our souls may be saved.

For Versicles the Sticheras of the resurrection, Tone 7.

Thou hast arisen from the grave, O Saviour of the world, and with Thy flesh hast Thou raised men; O Lord, glory to Thee.

Other Sticheras in alphabetical order.

Come, let us adore Him Who hath risen from the dead and enlightened all; for He hath delivered us from the tyranny of the hades, having by His resurrection on the third day bestowed on us life and great mercy.

Having descended into the hades, Thou hast, O Christ, made death captive, and, having arisen on the third day, Thou hast raised together with Thyself us also who glorify Thine all-powerful resurrection, O Lord—Lover of man.

Terrible didst Thou appear, O Lord, whilst lying in the grave as One-sleeping, and having arisen on the third day as Powerful, Thou hast raised, together with Thyself, Adam that was crying out: Glory to Thy resurrection, O only Lover of man.

Glory ... Both now ... The Theotokion:

Running for refuge under thine, O Sovereign-Lady, shelter we all the earth-born cry out unto thee: O Theotokos, our hope, deliver us from innumerable transgressions and save our souls.

The Troparion of the resurrection, Tone 7 :

Thou didst by Thy cross destroy death, to the malefactor hast opened paradise, unto the myrrh-bearing women hast changed the lamentation, and to the apostles hast commanded to proclaim that Thou art risen, O Christ the God, granting to the world great mercy.

Glory ... Both now ... The Theotokion :

As the treasury of our resurrection, do thou, O all-hymned one, lead up from the pit and abyss of transgressions those that trust in thee, for thou hast saved those that were guilty of sin, having given birth to our Salvation, O thou that wast Virgin both before and at child-birth, and remainedst still Virgin after the birth also.

At the Matins, after the 1*st Stichologia, the Cathismata of the resurrection. Tone* 7.

The Life was lying in the grave and the seal resting upon the stone, whilst soldiers were guarding Christ, as a King asleep, and angels were glorifying Him as God Immortal, whilst the women were calling out: Risen is the Lord granting unto the world great mercy.

O Christ the Lord, Who hast with Thy burial of three days made death captive and with Thy life-bearing awaking raised the corrupted man, as Lover of man,—glory to Thee.

Glory ... Both now ... The Theotokion :

Christ, our God, that was crucified for our sake and risen and hath destroyed the dominion of death, do thou, O Theotokos-Virgin, incessantly implore to save our souls.

After the 2*nd Stichologia, the Cathismata of the resurrection. Tone* 7.

Whilst the tomb was sealed, Thou didst as the Life arise from the grave, O Christ the God, and, whilst the doors were closed, Thou didst appear as the Resurrection of all unto Thy disciples,

« renewing through them within us a right Spirit according to Thy great mercy.*

To the tomb ran the women with tears, carrying spices, and whilst soldiers were guarding Thee—the King of all—thus spake unto one another: Who will roll off for us the stone? Risen is the Angel of the Great Council, having overthrown death. O Lord, All-powerful, glory to Thee.

Glory ... Both now ... The Theotokion:

Hail thou, full of grace, O Theotokos-Virgin, the haven and protection of the human race, since of thee was incarnate the Redeemer of the world, for thou alone art Mother and Virgin, ever-blessed and most glorious. Entreat Christ the God to grant peace unto all the universe.

The Hypakoe, Tone 7.

Thou that didst take to Thyself our form and endure the cross bodily, do save me by Thy resurrection, O Christ the God, as Lover of man.

The Graduals, Tone 7. Antiphon 1.

Having turned the captivity of Zion from deception,† do Thou, O Saviour, vivify me also, delivering me from the thraldom of passions.

In the south he that soweth afflictions of fasting with tears, will reap joyful handfuls of nutriment of life eternal.‡ [*Glory...*

With the Holy Spirit is the source of the divine treasures; from Him cometh wisdom, intelligence, fear; unto Him appertain praise and glory, honour and dominion.

Both now...the same. Antiphon 2.

Except the Lord build the house of the soul, in vain do we labour§; for but for Him neither deed nor word are accomplished.

---

* The Troparion of the holy apostle Thomas. † Psalm 125, 1.
‡ Psalm 125, 5. 6. § Psalm 126, 1.

Of the Fruit of the womb* the adopted children, the holy ones, moved by the Spirit, sprout forth traditions of the fathers. [*Glory...*

Of the Holy Spirit everything that is hath the existence, for He, before all, is God, hath Lordship over everything, is Light inaccessible, Life of all. [*Both now...the same. Antiphon* 3.

Those that fear the Lord, having found the ways of Life, are now and for ever blessed with immortal glory.†

Seeing round about thy table like the olive-branches thy children,‡ rejoice and be glad, bringing these unto Christ—the Chief Shepherd. [*Glory...*

With the Holy Spirit are abundance of gifts, riches of glory, of decrees great depth; He is of equal glory with the Father and the Son, for He hath service rendered unto Him.

Both now...the same. The Prokeimenon, Tone 7.

Arise, O Lord, my God, let Thy hand be lifted up, forget not Thy poor unto end. *The Verse:* I will confess unto Thee, O Lord, with my whole heart (Psalm 9, 33. 2).

The Canon of the resurrection. Tone 7. *Ode* 1. *The Heirmos:*

At Thy wink, O Lord, the nature of water, formerly easily diffusible, became changed into terrestrial form; wherefore, having walked dryshod, Israel singeth unto Thee an ode of victory.

By tree was condemned the tyranny of death, when Thou, O Lord, wast sentenced unto unrightful death: whereupon the prince of darkness, failing to overpower Thee, was rightfully driven away.

The hades did approach Thee and, having in vain tried to grind down Thy body with his teeth, hath broken his own jaws; whereupon, having done away with the dolours of death, Thou, O Saviour, hast arisen on the third day. [*The Theotokion:*

The sorrows of the first mother Eve have been done away with; for, having escaped sorrows, thou hast given birth without knowing a man; whereupon, manifestly acknowledging thee, O all-pure one, as Theotokos, we all glorify thee.

---

* Psalm 126, 3. † Psalm 127, 1. ‡ Psalm 127, 4.

Another Canon of the cross and resurrection. Tone 7. Ode I. The Heirmos: With the sea didst Thou cover Pharaoh and his chariots......

Two life-bearing fountains hath the Saviour on the cross made to flow unto us from His pierced side. Let us sing unto Him, for He is glorified.

Having dwelled in the grave and arisen on the third day, Christ hath granted unto the mortals a pledge of incorruption. Let us sing unto Him, for He is glorified. [*The Theotokion:*

Thou alone hast appeared Virgin after child-birth also, for thou hast brought forth incarnate the Maker of the world; wherefore we all call unto thee: Hail!

Another Canon to the all-holy Theotokos. Tone 7. The Heirmos: At Thy wink, O Lord...

Thou that hast brought forth Abyss of compassion, O Virgin, do illumine my soul with thy light-bearing brightness, that I may worthily hymn the abyss of thy wonders.

Seeing us wounded with a dart of sin, the Word as Benefactor hath taken compassion on us; whereupon the Most Divine One hath ineffably united Himself with the flesh that was of thee, O all-pure one.

The corrupt and mortal nature of man hath been seized by death, O Sovereign-Lady; but thou, having conceived the Life, hast from corruption unto life brought it up.

The Catabasis: I will open my mouth... *Ode 3. The Heirmos:*

Thou that in the beginning hast through Thine All-powerful Word—the heavens and through All-perfecting and Divine Spirit—all their power established, do Thou, O Lord—Saviour, stablish me upon the immoveable rock of Thy confession.

Ascending upon the tree, Thou voluntarily sorroweth for us, O Compassionate Saviour, and dost endure the wound capable of interceding for conciliation and salvation unto the faithful, whereby we all have become reconciled unto Thine, O Merciful One, Begetter.

My soul having been wounded by the bite of the serpent, Thou, O Christ, hast cleansed me from the sore and shewn light unto me who was of old lying low both in darkness and corruption; for, having descended through cross into the hades, Thou hast raised me up together with Thyself.

[*The Theotokion :*

Through the supplications of Thy Mother that hath known no man, do bestow, O Saviour, peace upon the world and unto the Emperor grant victory over inimical barbarians, and make worthy of Thine unspeakable glory those who doxologize Thee.

Another, the Heirmos : He that hath stablished heavens by the Word ...

Thou that hast endured sufferings on the cross and opened paradise unto the malefactor, as Benefactor and God, do Thou stablish my mind in Thy will, O Only-Lover of man.

Thou that hast risen from the grave on the third day and made life to shine on the world, as Life-Giver and God, do Thou stablish my mind in Thy will, O Only-Lover of man.

The Theotokion : Having without seed conceived God and freed Eve from the curse, do entreat, O Virgin-Mother Mariam, of thee incarnate God to save thy flock.

Another, the Heirmos: Thou that in the beginning hast ...

The creeping serpent of Eden having seduced me with the desire of deification, hath hurled me on earth, but the Merciful One and by nature Compassionate, taking pity on me hath deified me, having dwelled in thy womb and been like unto me, O Mother Virgin.

Blessed is the Fruit of thy womb, O Virgin-Theotokos, the joy of all; for thou hast brought forth unto all the world joy and true delight that driveth away sorrow of sin, O God's Bride.

Life Eternal and Light, O God's parent Virgin, and Peace hast thou brought forth unto us that calmeth the ancient enmity of men against the Father and God through faith and confession of the grace.

Ode 4. *The Heirmos :*

Without forsaking the bosom of Thy Father, Thou didst come down to the earth, O Christ the God ; the mystery of Thine economy I have heard and glorified Thee, O Only-Lover of man.

The slave having sinned, He that was incarnate of the Virgin giveth His own back for stripes and the innocent Master suffereth maltreatment, doing away with my transgressions.

Standing before the judgment-seat of the lawless judges, He that as God hath fashioned man and judgeth the earth rightfully is found guilty as one convicted and is boxed with fragile hand.

The Theotokion : As true Mother of God, do thou, all-spotless one, supplicate thy Maker and Son to lead me unto the saving haven of His glorious will.

Another, the Heirmos : The prophet perceiving ...

Not knowing sin and on its account having become, O Lord, what Thou wast not, Thou assumest form, having taken up foreign substance, that Thou mayest save the world and slay the tyrant by tempting him.

Upon the cross wast Thou lifted up and the sin of the first parent Adam hast Thou done away with (wherein I have heard Thy power), for Thou art come to save all Thine anointed.

The Theotokion : Thou born of the Virgin diest, but revivifiest Adam who hath erred in his judgment ; for death was afraid of Thy strength, seeing that Thou art come to save all the corrupted.

Another, the Heirmos : Without forsaking the bosom of Thy Father ...

O thou that hast appeared unto God before creation as one elect of all and good on account of the brightness of thine illumination, all-hymned one, do enlighten those that hymn thee.

God incarnate of thy pure blood and delivering from many sins hast thou, O pure one, brought forth unto men, that lovingly glorify and honour thee, O Mother-Virgin.

Unto Him Who shone forth from thee, O all-hymned one, doth perform sacred acts intelligent nature, having been now taught the mystery of thine unspeakable child-birth, O most blessed one.

Ode 5. *The Heirmos:*

Dark is the night to unbelievers, O Christ, but unto the faithful there is illumination in the delight of Thy words; wherefore unto Thee I watch early and hymn Thy Divinity.

For Thy slaves becomest Thou sold, O Christ, and blows on Thy cheek endurest that are instrumental in the deliverance of those who sing: Unto Thee I watch early and hymn Thy Divinity.

Through Thy divine power, O Christ, Thou hast in the infirmity of flesh overpowered the strong one, and in the resurrection hast Thou, O Saviour, shewn me a vanquisher of death. [*The Theotokion:*

God hast thou brought forth, O pure Mother, that was God-beseemingly incarnate of thee, O all-hymned one; since thou hast known no man, but barest of the Holy Spirit.

Another, the Heirmos: O Lord my God...

When, accounted among the lawless, wast Thou lifted up on Calvary, the luminaries hid themselves, the earth trembled and brightness of the temple was torn asunder, shewing the apostasy of the Jews.

We glorify in hymns Thee that hast destroyed the entire dominion of the tyrant by the strength of Thine incomprehensible Divinity, and hast raised the dead by Thy resurrection.

The Theotokion: O Mother of the King and God, all-hymned Theotokos, do thou send down, through thy supplications, deliverance from sins unto those who in faith and with love ever glorify thee in hymns.

Another, the Heirmos: Dark is the night to unbelievers...

Seeing a ladder fixed high above, Jacob did learn the image of thee that knewest not a man; for through thee God hath become united unto men, O all-pure Sovereign-Lady.

Having now found through thee, O Virgin, eternal deliverance we ardently cry unto thee: Hail thou, O God's Bride, and rejoicing in thy sight, O all-hymned one, we praise thee in songs.

The Bridegroom having found thee among thorns as the only lily, O Virgin, that wast shining with the lustre of purity and the light of virginity, O all-spotless one, hast accepted thee as a bride.

Ode 6. *The Heirmos:*

Swimming on the billows of the cares of life, sinking through the shipload of sins and thrown over to the soul-corrupting beast, as Jonah I cry unto thee, O Christ: Out of the mortiferous depth do bring me up.

The souls imprisoned in the hades and those of the remaining righteous remembered Thee and of Thee prayed for salvation, which Thou, O Christ, didst grant through the cross, having come down to those in the nethermost parts, as Compassionate One.

Thy living and not made by the hand of man Temple which was destroyed by the passion the choir of apostles hath despaired to again look upon, but having above all hope adored Thee, hath everywhere preached Thee as Risen One.

The Theotokion:

Of thine ineffable, all-spotless for our sake bringing forth the manner—who of men, O Virgin-God's Bride, is able to explain? for the Word having united Himself unto thee, the uncircumscribed God was made flesh of thee.

Another, the Heirmos: Jonah out of the belly...

Having been voluntarily lifted up on the cross, O Saviour, Thou hast made captive the dominion of the enemy, since Thou hast nailed to the cross the handwriting of the sin, O Good One.

Having risen from the dead with authority, Thou hast, O Saviour, raised together with Thyself the race of men, granting life and incorruption unto us, O Lover of Man.

[*The Theotokion:*

Do not cease, O Theotokos, importuning our God Whom thou hast ineffably brought forth that may be delivered from dangers those who hymn thee, O pure Ever-Virgin.

Another, the Heirmos: Swimming on the billows...

Types of the law and prophetic predictions have clearly pre-announced thee as one about to bring forth the Benefactor of all creation Who hath, O pure one, many times and in divers ways, done good unto those who in faith hymn thee.

Adam the first-fashioned who of old was driven away, through the slander of the man-slayer, from the divine delight of paradise, thou that knewest no man, hast again reinstated, having brought forth Him Who hath delivered us from transgression.

He that hath, by divine will and fashioning power, made everything from non-existing elements, is come from thine, O pure one, womb, and hath, with lightnings proceeding from God, enlightened those in the darkness of death.

The Contakion, Tone 7 :

No longer is the dominion of death capable of keeping men captive; for Christ hath come down, demolishing and destroying the power thereof; bound is now hades, the prophets rejoice saying with one voice: The Saviour hath appeared unto those that are in the state of belief; come out, O ye faithful, unto the resurrection. [*The Oikos :*

To-day the nethermost—the hades and death—have trembled below in the presence of One of the Trinity, the earth quaked and the gate-keepers of the hades were terrified at the sight of Thee, whereas the whole creation, together with the prophets, joyfully singeth an ode of victory unto Thee, the Redeemer, our God, Who hast now destroyed the power of death. Let us shout for joy and cry unto Adam and unto his descendants: A tree hath again brought him in; come out, O ye faithful, unto the resurrection.

Ode 7. *The Heirmos:*

The youths of old have the flaming furnace as dew-yielding shewn, since therein they were hymning One God and saying: O Most exalted God of the fathers and Most glorious.

By tree is Adam slain, having voluntarily committed disobedience, and by Christ's obedience is again renewed, for for my sake is crucified the Son of God, the Most Glorious.

Thee risen from the tomb the whole creation hath sung, O Christ, for Thou hast blossomed life unto those in the hades, resurrection unto the dead and unto those in darkness—light the most glorious.

The Theotokion: Hail thou, daughter of Adam the corrupted; Hail thou, God's only bride; Hail thou, through whom the corruption hath been driven away, who hath brought forth God. Him importune, O pure one, that we all may be saved.

Another, the Heirmos: Into the burning furnace thrown...

Thou that upon the tree of the cross the sting of sin hast blunted and destroyed the handwriting of Adam's transgression with the spear in Thy side, blessed art Thou, O Lord, the God of our fathers.

Thou that wast pierced in Thy side and with the sprinkling of Thy divine blood hast cleansed the earth which was polluted with the blood of idols' rage—blessed art Thou, O Lord, the God of our fathers.

Thou, O Mother of God, hast beamed forth unto the world illumination above that of the sun, even Christ Who doth deliver from darkness and enlighten with the knowledge of God all those that call out: Blessed art Thou, the God of our fathers.

Another, The Heirmos: The youths of old have the flaming furnace...

Thee, O Virgin, possessing ornaments of gold and wrought about with divers colours, did love thy Maker and Lord, the Most exalted God of the fathers and Most glorious.

Having taken the coal, Isaiah of old was cleansed,* symbolically seeing thy birth of the Most exalted God of the fathers and Most glorious.

Seeing the symbols of thy divine child-birth, the divine prophets of old joyfully hymning called out: O Most exalted God of the fathers and Most glorious.

Ode 8. *The Heirmos:*

The bush on Sinai, burning with fire, yet unconsumed, made God known unto the slow of speech and stuttering Moses, and God's zeal hath shewn the three youths in the fire unhurt and singing: Hymn the Lord, all ye the works of the Lord, and exalt Him unto all the ages.

Having been slain for the world, the unpolluted, intellectual Lamb hath made to cease the offerings prescribed by law, since, as God, He hath, besides errors, purified the latter, that for ever calleth out: Hymn the Lord, all ye the works of the Lord, and exalt Him unto all the ages.

Our flesh that was taken up by the Creator being before the passion not uncorrupted, after the passion and resurrection hath been made inaccessible to corruption and reneweth the mortals that call out: Hymn the Lord, all ye the works of the Lord, and exalt Him unto all the ages. [*The Theotokion:*

Thy purity and all-spotlessness, O Virgin, hath cleansed the universe of all filth and abomination, and thou wast the cause of our reconciliation with God, O all-pure one; wherefore thee, O Virgin, we with all the works bless and exalt unto all the ages.

Another, the Heirmos: Of the one unoriginate King...

Him that hath voluntarily endured the passion and was by His own will nailed on the cross and destroyed the powers of the hades,—hymn, O ye priests, and ye people, exalt unto all the ages.

Him that hath abolished the dominion of death and arisen in glory from the grave and saved the race of man,—hymn, O ye priests, and ye people, exalt unto all the ages. [*The Theotokion:*

---

* Isaiah 6, 6. 7.

The Only-compassionate, Eternal Word, that was at last born of the Virgin and did away with the ancient curse,—hymn, O ye priests, and ye people, exalt unto all the ages.

Another the Heirmos: The bush on Sinai, burning with fire...

With the light of thy child-birth hast thou, O God's Mother, in a strange way illumined the universe, for in thine arms thou carriest the Very God Who enlighteneth the faithful, ever calling out: Hymn the Lord, all ye the works of the Lord, and exalt Him unto all the ages.

We hymn piously thy womb that contained the God ineffably incarnate, Who hath bestowed the enlightenment of God's knowledge upon all the faithful ever calling out: Hymn the Lord, all ye the works of the Lord, and exalt Him unto all the ages.

With the flashes of thy light hast thou, O pure Theotokos, that broughtest forth the Light, made resplendent those that hymn thee; for thou didst appear as the Light's abode enlightening those that call out: Hymn the Lord, all ye the works of the Lord, and exalt Him unto all the ages.

Ode 9. *The Heirmos:*

Thou that without experiencing corruption gavest birth and unto the greatest Artificer—the Word—hast lent out flesh, O Mother that knewest not a man, O Virgin-Theotokos, container of the Illimitable, abode of the Infinite, thy Fashioner,—thee we magnify.

Shut your mouths, all ye otherwise-minded that make passion applicable to the Deity; for the Lord of glory crucified in flesh and not in the divine substance, as One in two substances,—we glorify.

Going unto Christ's tomb, learn all ye who do not believe in the rising of the bodies that the flesh of the Life-giver was put to death and arisen again, in assurance of the last resurrection, which we hope for.

Of the Trinity: Honouring neither the Trinity of Deities, but of Hypostases, nor the Unity of Persons, but of Godhead, we cut off those who divide It, and yet again we overthrow those who dare to confound It Whom we magnify.

Another, the Heirmos: O Mother of God and Virgin...

Light of Light, Effulgence of the Father's glory, glittering without times, Christ shone forth unto the human life as if in darkness and drove away the persecuting darkness; Him we the faithful do unceasingly magnify.

Let those who, seeing in Christ passions of flesh and strength of divinity, believe in one compound nature be confounded; for it is as man He dieth and as the Maker of everything ariseth.

Myrrh unto the dead, but unto the Living One a hymn, unto the dying tears and unto the Life of all a joyful song do bring, O ye women,—cried out the preacher of the awaking, announcing Christ's resurrection.

Beside Thee I do not know of any God, crieth out the Church; from the unfaithful nations hast Thou selected me as Thy bride. Grant then, O Word, as Compassionate, salvation unto the faithful, through the intercession of her that bare Thee.

Another, the same Heirmos:

Of eternal gladness and joy mediatrix hast thou appeared for us, O Ever-virgin, Maiden, having brought forth the Redeemer,—unto those who in truth and divine spirit honour Him as the redeeming God.

David, thine ancestor, O all-pure one, psalmodizing, nameth thee an ark of divine holiness* that supernaturally contained God sitting in the bosom of the Father, Whom we the faithful unceasingly magnify.

Inasmuch as thou art truly above all nature, O Maiden, for the Creator of all hast thou brought forth in flesh unto us; therefore as Mother of the One Master thou bringest the primary overcoming against all.

With the Lauds the Sticheras of the resurrection, Tone 7.

Christ is risen from the dead, having destroyed the bonds of death; proclaim, O earth, great joy; laud, O heavens, God's glory.

---

* Psalm 131, 8.

Having beheld the resurrection of Christ, let us adore the Holy Lord Jesus, the only sinless.

We do not cease adoring the resurrection of Christ, for He hath saved us from our iniquities,—the Holy Lord Jesus that hath shewn the resurrection.

What shall we render unto the Lord for all things which He hath done unto us? For our sake was God among men; on account of the corrupted nature the Word became flesh and dwelled in us; unto ungrateful He is Benefactor unto captives their Deliverer, unto those sitting in darkness—the Sun of righteousness, on the cross—the Impassible, in the hades—Light, in death—Life, Resurrection for the sake of the fallen. Let us cry out unto Him: O our God, glory to Thee.

Other, Anatolian Sticheras, the same Tone:

Gates of the hades hast Thou, O Lord, destroyed and the dominion of death abolished by Thy mighty power, and together with Thyself raised the dead that were for ages sleeping in darkness, by Thy divine and glorious resurrection, as the King of all and God All-powerful.

Come, let us exult in the Lord and rejoice on account of His resurrection, for He hath raised with Himself the dead that were held by the indestructible bonds in the hades, and hath bestowed upon the world life everlasting and great mercy.

Shining angel sat on the stone of Thy life-bearing tomb and announcing unto the myrrh-bearing women glad tidings said: Risen is the Lord, as He told you before; announce to the disciples that He will meet you in Galilee; and unto the world He granteth life eternal and great mercy.

Why have ye neglected the Chief Corner-stone, O most wicked Jews? He it is Whom God hath laid in Zion, Who in the wilderness made water to flow from a stone* and causeth immortality to flow unto us from His side; this is the Stone that was cut off from the virginal mount without man's

---

* Exodus, 17, 6. Numbers 20, 11.

desire *; He is the Son of man coming on the clouds of heaven to the Ancient of days, as Daniel hath said, and His Kingdom is everlasting.†

In the Liturgy with the Beatitudes, Tone 7.

Pleasing to the eyes and good for food was the fruit that hath slain me, and Christ is the Tree of life eating of which I do not die, but cry out with the malefactor: Remember me, O Lord, in Thy Kingdom.

Having been lifted up on the cross, O Compassionate One, Thou hast obliterated the handwriting of Adam's ancient sin and saved the whole race of man from illusion, wherefore we hymn Thee, O Benefactor, Lord.

Thou hast nailed to the cross, O Compassionate One, our sins, and by Thy death slain death, O Christ, having raised the dead from death; wherefore we adore Thy holy resurrection.

The serpent hath once poured the poison into the ears of Eve, and Christ hath on the tree of the cross made to flow into the world the sweetness of life; wherefore we cry out: Remember us, O Lord, in Thy Kingdom.

Into the tomb as dead one wast Thou laid, O Life of all, Christ, and Thou hast shattered the door-posts of the hades and having, as Powerful, risen on the third day in glory, Thou hast enlightened all; glory to Thine awaking.

The Lord having risen from the dead on the third day, hath bestowed peace upon His disciples, and having blessed them, hath sent them saying: Bring all into My Kingdom.

[*Glory...of the Trinity:*

Light is the Father, Light is the Son and Word, Light is the Holy Spirit; but the Three are One Light, for One is God in Three Persons, but in one substance and origin, Indivisible and not to be confounded, the One Ever-existing.

[*Both now...the Theotokion:*

Thou hast brought forth upon earth the Son and Word of

---

* Dan. 2, 34. 45. † Dan, 7, 13.

the Father in flesh, as He Himself, O Theotokos, knoweth; wherefore, being deified by thee, O Virgin-Mother, we call unto thee: Hail thou, the hope of the Christians.

The Prokeimenon, Tone 7: The Lord shall give strength unto His people, the Lord shall give His people the blessing of peace. *The Verse:* Bring unto the Lord, O ye sons of God, bring young rams unto the Lord (*Psalm* 28, 11, 1).

Alleluia: It is good to confess to the Lord, and to offer psalmody to Thy name, O Most High. *The Verse:* To proclaim Thy mercy in the morning and Thy truth every night.

ON SATURDAY, AT THE GREAT VESPERS.

For "O Lord, I have cried" the Sticheras of the resurrection, Tone 8.

Vespertine hymn and intellectual service we offer unto Thee, O Christ, since Thou wast pleased to have mercy on us through the resurrection.

O Lord, Lord, do not cast us away from Thy presence, but be pleased to have mercy on us through the resurrection.

Hail thou, O holy Zion, mother of churches, God's abode, for thou wast the first to obtain remission of sins through the resurrection.

Other, Anatolian Sticheras. Tone 8:

The Word, that before the ages of God the Father was begotten and at the end of times became voluntarily incarnate of the one who did not know marital life,—hath endured deadly crucifixion and hath saved by His own resurrection the man that was slain of old.

We glorify Thy resurrection from the dead, O Christ, by which Thou hast delivered Adam's race from the tyranny of the hades and bestowed upon the world, as God, life eternal and great mercy.

Glory to Thee, O Christ-Saviour, Son of God the Only-begotten, that wast nailed on the cross and arisen from the grave on the third day.

Thee, O Lord, we glorify, Who for our sake hast voluntarily endured the cross, and Thee we adore, O All-powerful Saviour; do not cast us away from Thy presence, but hearken and save us by Thy resurrection, O Lover of man.

Glory...Both now...The Theotokion :

The King of the heavens, for the sake of love to man, hath appeared on earth and lived among men; for the Son that hath of the pure Virgin taken flesh and come from her together with what He hath taken, is One, twofold of nature but not in hypostasis; wherefore preaching of Him as truly perfect God and perfect man, we confess Christ as our God. Him supplicate, O Mother unmarried, that our souls may be saved.

For Versicles the Sticheras of the resurrection, Tone 8.

Thou hast ascended the cross, O Christ, having come down from heaven; Thou camest unto death as Life immortal, unto those in darkness as true Light, unto the fallen as the Resurrection of all; O Enlightenment and our Saviour, glory to Thee.

Other Sticheras, in alphabetical order :

Let us doxologize Christ risen from the dead; for having taken both soul and body, He hath cut off the passions of both, since the unpolluted soul hath descended into the hades and made it captive, and in the grave hath not seen corruption the holy body of the Deliverer of our souls.

In psalmodies and hymns we doxologise Thine, O Christ, resurrection from the dead, by which Thou hast delivered us from the tyranny of the hades, and as God bestowed on us life eternal and great mercy.

O Master of all, incomprehensible Maker of heaven and earth! Having suffered on the cross Thou hast made immortality to flow unto me, and having submitted to the burial and risen in glory, Thou hast raised Adam together with Thyself, by Thine all powerful arm. Glory to Thine arising on the third day, whereby Thou hast granted unto us life eternal and expiation of sins, as the only Compassionate One.

[*Glory...Both now...The Theotokion:*

O Virgin unmarried, that hast ineffably conceived God in the flesh, O Mother of the Most High God! Do hearken unto the prayers of thy servants, O all-spotless one, that grantest unto all purification of transgressions; receiving now our supplications, importune that our souls may be saved.

The Troparion of the resurrection, Tone 8:

From on high didst Thou descend, O Tender-hearted One, hast submitted to the burial of three days that Thou mightest deliver us from our passions; our Life and Resurrection, O Lord, glory to Thee.

Thou that for our sake wast born of the Virgin and didst endure crucifixion, O Good One, Who by death hast, as God, overthrown death and made resurrection manifest, despise not those whom Thou hast fashioned with Thy hand; show forth Thy love to man, O Merciful One; receive the Theotokos that bare Thee, who intercedeth for us, and save, O Saviour, the despairing people.*

At the Matins, after the 1*st Stichologia, the Cathismata of the resurrection, Tone* 8.

Risen from the dead is the Life of all, and a bright angel cried out unto the women: stay your tears, announce good tidings to the apostles, cry out in song that risen is Christ the Lord, Who was pleased as God to save the race of men.

Having indeed arisen from the grave, Thou hast commanded unto the honourable women to announce Thine arising to the apostles, as it is written; and precipitous Peter stood at the tomb and observing light in the grave was terrified, but seeing also the wrappers lying therein without the divine body, and

---

* The Theotokion of the Ninth Hour.

believing he cried out: Glory to Thee, O Christ the God, that Thou savest all, O our Saviour, for Thou art the Effulgence of the Father. [*Glory...Both now...the Theotokion:*

Let us hymn the heavenly gate and ark, the all-holy mount, the resplendent cloud, the heavenly ladder, the rational paradise, the redemption of Eve, the great treasure of the whole universe, since in her was accomplished salvation of the world and remission of the ancient sins; wherefore we cry out unto thee: Intercede before thy Son and God that He may grant remission of transgressions unto those that piously adore thine all-holy child-birth.

After the 2nd Stichologia, the Cathismata of the resurrection, Tone 8.

Men, O Saviour, have sealed Thy tomb; angel hath rolled the stone off the door; women did see Thee risen from the dead and have announced unto Thy disciples in Zion that Thou hast arisen, O Life of all, and the bonds of death were loosed; O Lord, glory to Thee.

The women having brought the burial-spices, heard an angel's voice coming from the grave: Stay your tears and instead of sorrow receiving gladness, cry out in song that risen is Christ Who was pleased as God to save the race of men.

[*Glory...Both now...the Theotokion:*

In thee, O full of grace, rejoiceth all the creation, the body of angels and the race of men, O thou hallowed temple and rational paradise, glory of virgins, of whom God was incarnate and became a little child, our God that is before the ages; for thy womb He made into a throne and thy belly He rendered wider than the heavens. In thee, O full of grace, rejoiceth all the creation, glory to thee.*

The Hypakoe, Tone 8:

The myrrh-bearing women, standing at the tomb of the Life-giver, sought the Master, the Immortal One, among the dead,

---

* Instead of "It is truly meet to bless Thee," in the Liturgy of St. Basil the Great this hymn is used.

and having received from the angel the glad tidings of joy, announced unto the apostles that Christ the Lord is risen granting unto the world great mercy.

The Graduals, Tone 8. *Antiphon* 1:

From my youth up* the enemy tempteth me, burneth me with the delights; but trusting in Thee, O Lord, I triumph over him.

Let those that hate Zion be as the grass before it is plucked up; for Christ will pare away their necks† with the cutting of torments. [*Glory*...

Of the Holy Spirit is everything unto life; as Light of Light He is Great God; Him we hymn together with the Father and the Word.

Both now...the same. Antiphon 2:

Let my heart be humbly minded covered with fear of Thee, lest becoming conceited it fall away from Thee, O All-compassionate One‡.

He that trusteth in the Lord§ will not be terrified at the time when He will have to judge all with fire and torment. [*Glory*...

Of the Holy Spirit inspired, every one who beholdeth and foresheweth doth great marvels, singing in the Three One God, for, although the Divinity triply shineth, It hath One Origin only.

Both now...the same. Antiphon 3:

I have called unto Thee, O Lord, hearken to me, incline Thine ear to me when I cry|| and cleanse me before Thou takest me hence.

Returning back unto his mother-earth, every one becometh again decomposed to receive either punishments or rewards for his life. [*Glory*...

Of the Holy Spirit is the theology: Thrice-holy Unity; for the Father is Unoriginate, of Whom, without times, was born

---

* Psalm 128, 1-2. † Psalm, 128, 6. 4. ‡ Psalm 130, 2. 1. § Psalm 130, 3. || Psalm 129, 1-2.

the Son and the Co-throned, Co-formed Spirit Who also shone forth from the Father.

Both now...the same. Antiphon 4.

Behold now, what is good and delightful but for brethren to live together in unity*; for therein the Lord promised life everlasting.

For one's raiment He that adorneth the lilies of the field, enjoineth that it behoveth not to take thought.† [*Glory:*

Of the Holy Spirit, as of one uniform cause, everything is held and obtaineth peace, for He is God, of one lordly substance with the Father and the Son.

Both now...the same. The Prokeimenon, Tone 8.

The Lord shall reign for ever, thy God, O Zion, from generation to generation.

The Verse: Praise the Lord, O my soul; I will praise the Lord in my life (Psalm 145, 10. 1).

The Canon of the resurrection, Tone 8. *Ode* 1. *The Heirmos:*

The pursuing Pharaoh with the chariots did once submerge the cruciformly stretched and dividing the sea miraculous rod of Moses, but it hath saved fugitive Israel, who proceeded on foot singing a chant unto God.

At the all-powerful Divinity of Christ—how can we help wondering? Since from the passion it maketh impassibility and incorruption to flow unto all the faithful, and from the holy side—fount of immortality to spring, and from the grave—life everlasting.

How beautiful unto the women hath the angel now appeared, bearing luminous attributes of the innate immaterial purity, and with the countenance announcing the light of the resurrection, whilst calling out: Risen is the Lord. [*The Theotokion:*

Glorious things began to be said from generation unto generation of thee, O Theotokos-Virgin, thou hast contained in thy womb God the Word and remained pure; wherefore we all honour thee as, after God, our protection.

---

* Psalm 132, 1. † Matth. 6, 28.

The Canon of the cross and resurrection. The Heirmos : Having crossed water as dry land...

Lifted were the dolorous gates and frightened the gate-keepers of the hades, beholding the descent into the nethermost parts of One Who is the highest of all, above nature.

Amazed were the angelic orders, beholding seated on the throne of the Father the fallen human nature that was shut up in the nethermost parts of the earth.

The orders both of angels and men do unceasingly praise thee, O unmarried Mother, for their Maker as an infant in thine arms hast thou borne.

Another Canon of the all-holy Theotokos.

The Heirmos : Let us chant unto the Lord that hath led His people through...

O most pure Theotokos, that hast the Incarnate, Ever-existing and Most Divine Word supernaturally brought forth, we hymn thee.

Thee, the life-bearing Cluster shedding the sweetness of the universal salvation, hath the Virgin brought forth, O Christ.

The race of Adam elevated unto the blessedness incomprehensible through thee, O Theotokos, doth worthily glorify thee.

The Catabasis : I will open my mouth ... *Ode* 3.
The Heirmos :

Thou that hast in the beginning stablished the heavens in wisdom and the earth founded upon the waters, do Thou, O Christ, stablish me upon the rock of Thy commandments,* for there is none holy but Thou, O Only Lover of man.

Adam condemned for sinful eating, with the saving passion of Thy body hast Thou, O Christ, set free, for Thyself wast Thou, O Sinless One, not guilty of the deadly charge.

The light of the resurrection hast Thou, O Jesus, my God, made to shine unto those sitting in darkness and in the shadow of death, and by Thy Divinity, having bound the strong one, his vessels hast Thou despoiled. [*The Theotokion :*

---

* Church.

Much higher than the cherubim and seraphim hast thou appeared, O Theotokos; for thou alone hast received the Boundless One in thy womb, O untainted one; wherefore we all the faithful in hymns call thee blessed, O pure one.

Another, the Heirmos: O Lord, the Roofer of the heavenly firmament...

Whilst I did once turn away from the commandment, Thou hast, O Lord, cast me away in disdain, but, having taken up my form and taught obedience, through crucifixion hast Thou implanted me again in Thyself.

Foreseeing everything in wisdom, O Lord, and in Thine intelligence having set up the nethermost regions, Thou didst not disdain by Thy descent, O Word of God, to raise him that is in Thine image. [*The Theotokion:*

Having dwelled bodily in the Virgin, Thou hast, O Lord, manifested Thyself unto men as it behoved to see Thee; her also hast Thou shewn as true Theotokos and help of the faithful, O Only Lover of man.

Another, the Heirmos: Thou art the strengthening...

Give us help with thy supplications, O all-pure one, that we may repulse the attacks of the terrible surroundings.

Unto Eve, the first mother, wast thou become rehabilitation, having brought forth Christ, the Author of the life of the world, O Theotokos.

Gird me about with dominion, O all-pure one, that hast truly brought forth God in flesh—Hypostatic Power of the Father.

Ode 4. *The Heirmos:*

Thou art my strength, O Lord, Thou also my power, Thou my God, Thou my exultation, since, without forsaking Thy Father's bosom, Thou hast also visited our wretchedness; wherefore with the prophet Habbakuk I call unto Thee: Glory to Thy power, O Lover of man.

Although Thine enemy, didst Thou exceedingly love me: by extraordinary emptying art Thou come down upon earth, O

Compassionate Saviour, not shunning even my last outrage, and whilst Thyself remaining on the height of Thine unspeakable glory, Thou hast glorified me, formerly disgraced.

Who is not astonished now beholding death being done away with? Corruption being driven away by the cross and the hades being emptied of its treasures by death through the divine authority of Thee the Crucified One,—it is a wonderful deed, O Lover of man! [*The Theotokion:*

Thou art the boast of the faithful, O unmarried Bride, thou art the protection and refuge of Christians, wall and haven; for unto thy Son dost thou bring supplications, O all-spotless one, and savest from dangers those who in faith and with love acknowledge thee as Theotokos, O pure one.

Another, the Heirmos: I have heard, O Lord...

On the cross have nailed Thee, O Christ the God, the children of the law-breakers, and thereby hast Thou, as Compassionate, saved those who glorify Thy passion.

Having risen from the tomb, Thou hast raised with Thyself the dead in the hades and enlightened, as Compassionate, those who glorify Thy resurrection. [*The Theotokion:*

The God Whom thou hast brought forth, O undefiled Mary, Him do supplicate to grant unto thy servants the forgiveness of sins.

Another, the same Heirmos:

O thou—unploughed field—who hast sprouted forth the life-causing Ear, that granteth life unto the world, save, O Theotokos, those who hymn thee.

As Theotokos do we all the enlightened proclaim thee, O all pure one, for thou hast brought forth the Sun of righteousness, O Ever-virgin.

Grant expiation unto our deeds of ignorance, as Sinless One, and pacify Thy world, O God, for the sake of intercessions of her who hath brought Thee forth.

Ode 5. *The Heirmos:*

Why hast Thou driven me away from Thy presence, O Light never-setting, and why hath covered me—the miserable one—the enemy's darkness? Do howbeit turn me and set my paths unto the light of Thy commandments—I pray Thee.

Thou hast suffered Thyself to be vested in purple-robe whilst being insulted just before Thy passion, O Saviour, in order to cover offensive nakedness of the first-fashioned one, and naked wast Thou nailed upon the cross, whilst pulling off, O Christ, the garment of death.

Out of mortal earth hast Thou again reconstructed my fallen nature, having arisen Thyself, and hast, O Christ, made it never-growing-old, having shewn it once more as a King's image shining with the light of immortality. [*The Theotokion:*

Possessing mother's boldness unto thy Son, do not neglect, we implore thee, O all-pure one, the care for thy race; for thee and thee alone do we Christians offer unto the Master for gracious propitiation.

Another, the Heirmos: Enlighten us......

Guide us with the power of Thy cross, O Christ, for therewith we fall down before Thee; Thy peace grant unto us, O Lover of man.

Pilot our life as All-good One,* since we hymn Thine awaking, and grant us peace, as Lover of man. [*The Theotokion:*

Persuade, O pure one, thy Son and our God, O chaste Mary, who knewest not marital life, that He may send down unto us, the faithful, great mercy.

Another, the Heirmos: Watching early we cry out unto Thee...

Tranquillize the intolerable tempest of my passions, O thou that hast brought forth God—the Pilot and Lord.

Unto thine Offspring, O undefiled Theotokos, serve angelic orders and assemblies of men, O Mary, Theotokos unmarried, do frustrate the designs of the enemies and gladden those who hymn thee.

---

* Our God.

Ode 6. The Heirmos.

Cleanse me, O Saviour, for my iniquities are many, and bring me up from the depth of the evil, I implore Thee : for unto Thee have I cried, do then hearken unto me, O God of my salvation.

By means of the tree mightily hath hurled me down the originator of evil, but Thou, O Christ, having been lifted on the cross, hast put down the powerful one, since Thou hast abashed him, and raised the fallen one.

Shining forth from the tomb Thou hast invigorated Zion, having, as Compassionate, accomplished her as new in place of old by Thy divine blood, and now dost Thou reign in her unto the ages, O Christ. [*The Theotokion :*

May we be freed from atrocious stumblings by thine entreaties, O pure parent of God, and may we, O all pure one, be vouchsafed to meet the divine effulgence of the Son of God Who was unspeakably incarnate of thee.

Another, the Heirmos: My prayer will I pour unto the Lord ...

Thy palms hast Thou spread upon the cross, healing the incontinently stretched hand of the first-fashioned one in Eden, and having of Thine own free will tasted gall, Thou, O Christ, hast saved, as Powerful, those who glorify Thy sufferings.

The Redeemer hath tasted death that He might do away with the reign of the ancient condemnation and corruption, and, having descended into the hades, Christ hath arisen and saved, as Mighty One, those who hymn His resurrection.

[*The Theotokion :*

Cease not interceding for us, O all-pure Theotokos-Virgin, for thou art the support of the faithful; by the hope in thee we become fortified and lovingly do we glorify thee and Him Who was ineffably incarnate of thee.

Another, the Heirmos : Grant unto me a bright garment...

As God's temple and ark, living palace and heaven's door, we the faithful proclaim thee, O Theotokos.

The Destroyer of heathen temples as God—thy former Offspring, O Mary—God's Bride, is adored together with the Father and the Holy Spirit.

The Word of God hath shewn thee unto those on earth to be a heavenly ladder, for through thee He did descend unto us.

The Contakion, Tone 8. *Similar to:* As the first fruits...

Being risen from the tomb, Thou hast made the dead alive and raised up Adam; Eve also is jubilant through Thy resurrection, and the ends of the world are triumphing on account of Thy rising from the dead, O Greatly Merciful One.

The Oikos:

Having captured the dominions of the hades and raised the dead, Thou, O Long-suffering, hast met the myrrh-bearing women bringing unto them gladness in the place of sorrow; unto apostles also hast Thou, O my Saviour, Giver of life, made known the symbols of victory, and dost enlighten the creation, O Lover of man; wherefore the world also doth participate in the joy on account of Thy rising from the dead, O Greatly Merciful One.

Ode 7. *The Heirmos:*

Through God's descent the fire in Babylon did once become softened; wherefore the youths, dancing with joyful step in the furnace as if it were a flowery lawn, sung: Blessed art Thou, O God of our fathers.

The glorious emptying, the divine abundance of Thy poverty doth amaze, O Christ, angels beholding Thee nailed to the cross in order to save those who in faith call out: Blessed art Thou, O God of our fathers.

By Thy divine descent, Thou hast filled with light the nethermost parts, and the darkness that did formerly torment was driven away; therefrom arose those that were in bonds for ages, calling out: Blessed art Thou, O God of our fathers.

Of the Trinity:

Orthodoxly theologizing we proclaim the Lord of all, Thee—the Sole Father of the Only-begotten Son, and acknowledge the One Rightful Spirit, proceeding from Thee, of the same nature and Co-eternal.

Another the Heirmos: From Judea coming...

Salvation hast Thou, O God, accomplished in the midst of the universe, according to the prophetic saying; for, having been lifted up on the tree, Thou hast called back all those that in faith cry out: O God of our fathers, blessed art Thou.

Having arisen from the grave as from sleep, Thou hast, O Compassionate, delivered all from corruption, and the creation is confirmed in faith by apostles preaching the awaking; O God of the fathers, blessed art Thou. [*The Theotokion:*

Of equal energy with the Begetter, of equal power and co-eternal, the Word, by the good will of the Father and the Spirit, is being created in the womb of the Virgin; O God of our fathers, blessed art Thou.

Another, the same Heirmos:

Having become incarnate in the virginal womb, Thou hast appeared for our salvation; wherefore acknowledging Thy Mother as Theotokos we orthodoxly call out: O God of the fathers, blessed art Thou.

Thou, O Virgin, hast sprouted forth a rod from the root of Jesse, O all-blessed one, a flower-bearing fruit saving unto those who in faith call out unto Thy Son: O God of the fathers, blessed art Thou.

O hypostatic wisdom of the Highest, do Thou fill with wisdom and divine power through the Theotokos all those who in faith psalmodize unto Thee: O God of our fathers, blessed art Thou.

Ode 8. *The Heirmos:*

Sevenfold hath the enraged Chaldean tyrant caused the furnace to be heated for the God-fearing, but seeing these saved by a better power, unto the Creator and Redeemer he cried out: Bless, O ye youths, hymn, O ye priests, ye people, exalt Him unto all the ages.

The hyperdivine power of the Divinity of Jesus hath shone forth in us God-beseemingly; for, having in flesh tasted death on the cross for all, He hath destroyed the stronghold of the hades; Him unceasingly bless, O ye children, hymn, O ye priests, ye people exalt Him unto all the ages.

The Crucified One arose, the braggart fell, the fallen and contrite one is re-established, the corruption is driven away and the incorruption hath blossomed; for by the Life everything deadly hath been swallowed up. Bless, O ye children, hymn, O ye priests, ye people, exalt Him unto all the ages.

[*Of the Trinity:*

The Thrice-luminous Godhead shining as one aurora from one three-hypostatical nature—the Begetter Unoriginate, the Word of the same nature as the Father and the Co-reigning Spirit of the same substance—bless, O ye children, hymn, O ye priests, and ye people, exalt unto all the ages.

Another, the Heirmos: The vanquishers of the tyrant...

Him that from the tree hath extended His arms unto me, the naked one, calling upon me to be covered with His beautiful nakedness,—bless, all ye the works of the Lord, and exalt Him unto the ages.

Him that hath raised me, fallen one, from the nethermost hades and hath honoured me with the high-throned glory of the Begetter,—bless the Lord, all ye the works of the Lord, and exalt Him unto the ages.

The Theotokion: Of Adam the fallen thou, O Virgin, hast appeared a daughter, but of God Who hath renewed my nature—Mother; Him we hymn with all the works, as Lord, and exalt unto all the ages.

Another, the Heirmos: The King of the Heavens...

Of the enemies the enchanting and inflaming arrows directed against us do thou destroy, that we may hymn thee, O pure one, unto all the ages.

Supernaturally hast thou, O Virgin, given birth to the Creator and Saviour—God the Word; wherefore we hymn thee and extol unto all the ages.

The Light Unapproachable having abided in thee, O Virgin, hath shewn thee as an illumining and gold-lustrous lamp unto all the ages.

Ode 9. The Heirmos:

Terrified was heaven and the ends of the earth were amazed that God hath bodily appeared unto men and that thy womb hath become more spacious than the heavens; wherefore thee, O Theotokos, the highest among angels and men magnify.

Being simple in Thy divine and unoriginate nature, Thou hast, O Christ the God, become compounded by taking up flesh, made within Thyself, O Word of God, and, having undergone sufferings as man, Thou didst remain foreign to passions as God; wherefore Thee in two substances undivided and unmixed we magnify.

The Father in His divine substance, Thou, being by nature a man, hast called God when Thou, O High One, didst descend unto Thy servants; having risen from the tomb, Thou hast presented unto the earthly Him Who is by nature God and Master as Father by grace; Thee with Him do we all magnify.

[*The Theotokion:*

Thou hast, O Virgin, appeared Mother of God, since thou didst bring forth in flesh God the Word, Whom the Father, in His goodness, before all ages, hath brought out of His heart, and Whom we now consider as above all bodies, although He hath put on the body.

Another, the Heirmos: Frightened was every hearing...

We acknowledge Thee as by nature the Son of God that wast conceived in the womb of the God's Mother, and hast become for our sake man, and beholding Thee on the cross suffering in Thy human nature and remaining impassible as God, we magnify Thee.

Destroyed was the ancient darkness, for out of the hades there arose the Sun of righteousness—even Christ, that enlighteneth all the ends of the earth, sparkling with the light of Divinity—heavenly man, God upon earth; Him in two natures we magnify.

Gird Thee, and prosper, and rule as King,* O Son of God's Mother, subjecting the Ishmaelitish nations that fight against

---

* Psalm 44, 5.

us, and to the heartily pious Emperor who hath recourse unto Thee, granting with the lance, as an invincible weapon, the cross.

Another, the Heirmos: As truly the Theotokos...

Thy memory filleth with joy and gladness, causing cures to flow unto those that have recourse unto thee and piously proclaim thee Theotokos.

In psalms we hymn thee, O full of grace, and unceasingly cry unto thee "Hail," for thou hast caused gladness to flow unto all.

Beautiful hath become, O Theotokos, thy Fruit, procuring not corruption but life unto those who participate thereof, and in faith magnify thee.

With the Lauds the Sticheras of the resurrection, Tone 8*:*

O Lord, although before the judgment-seat stoodest Thou being tried by Pilate, but Thou didst not step off the throne whereon Thou sitteth together with the Father, and, having arisen from the dead, Thou hast delivered the world from the thraldom of the enemy, as Compassionate One and Lover of man.

O Lord, a weapon against the devil hast Thou given us in Thy cross, for he quaketh and trembleth, unable to bear the sight of its might, since it raiseth the dead and hath abolished death; wherefore we adore Thy burial and awaking.

O Lord, although the Jews placed Thee in the grave as a Dead One, but as a King sleeping they caused soldiers to guard Thee and as the Treasury of life they secured with a seal; howbeit Thou hast arisen and granted incorruption unto our souls.

Thine angel, O Lord, preaching the resurrection, hath frightened the watchmen and unto the women called, saying: Why seek ye the Living One among the dead? Risen is He—the God—and unto the universe hath granted life.

Other, Eastern Sticheras, the same Tone:

Thou hast suffered on the cross, being impassible in the Divinity; Thou hast endured the burial of three days, that

Thou mightest deliver us from the thraldom of the enemy and, having made us immortal, revivify us, O Christ the God, by Thy resurrection, as Lover of man.

I adore, doxologize and hymn, O Christ, Thy resurrection from the grave, by which Thou hast freed us from the unbreakable chains of the hades and granted unto the world, as God, life eternal and great mercy.

Thy life-containing tomb guarding, the law-breakers sealed and set a watch over it; but Thou, as God Immortal and All-powerful, hast arisen on the third day.

When Thou, O Lord, hast reached the gates of the hades and shattered them, the captured one thus cried out: Who is This One that He not only is not condemned in the nethermost parts of the earth, but even hath as a shadow destroyed the prison of death? I received Him as a dead one and tremble before Him as God. O All-powerful Saviour, have mercy upon us.

In the Liturgy, with the Beatitudes, Tone 8:

Remember me, O Christ, Saviour of the world, as Thou didst remember the malefactor on the tree, and deign to make us all worthy of Thy heavenly Kingdom, as the only Compassionate One.

Hear, O Adam, and rejoice with Eve, that he who formerly made both naked, and hath through deceit carried you captives, is by the cross of Christ abolished.

Having been voluntarily nailed on a tree, Thou didst, O our Saviour, deliver Adam from the curse that was of a tree, restoring unto him, as Compassionate One, that which was in the image and the life in paradise.

To-day Christ was risen from the grave granting unto all the faithful incorruption, and after the passion and awaking He doth renew joy unto the myrrh-bearing women.

Rejoice, O ye wise myrrh-bearing women, that were the first to see the resurrection of Christ and to announce it unto the apostles—the recall of the whole world.

Having appeared as friends of Christ that are to be co-throned with Him in His glory, O ye apostles do, as His disciples, pray unto Him that we may with boldness stand before Him. [*Glory...of the Trinity :*

O Unoriginate Trinity, Undivided Substance, Co-throned Unity, of the same Glory, Nature and Sovereignty above all origin,—do save those that in faith hymn Thee.

[*Both now...The Theotokion :*

Hail thou, God's extensive receptacle; hail thou, ark of the new covenant; hail thou, the golden pot from which heavenly Manna was given unto all.

The Prokeimenon, Tone 8 :

Pray and render unto the Lord our God. *The Verse:* In Judea is God known, in Israel great is His name (Psalm 75, 12. 2).

Alleluia: O come, let us rejoice unto the Lord, let us shout unto the God, our Saviour. *The Verse:* Let us come before His presence with confessions and shout to Him in psalms (Psalm 94, 1-2).

Column I of the matutinal Gospels beginneth with the first Sunday in the Lent of SS. Peter and Paul.

Tone 1, *the Gospel of the resurrection* 2	*Tone* 5, *the Gospel of the resurrection* 6
Tone 2, *the Gospel of the resurrection* 3	*Tone* 6, *the Gospel of the resurrection* 7
Tone 3, *the Gospel of the resurrection* 4	*Tone* 7, *the Gospel of the resurrection* 8
Tone 4, *the Gospel of the resurrection* 5	*Tone* 8, *the Gospel of the resurrection* 9

Column II of the matutinal Gospels commenceth after the Feast of Elijah.

Tone 1, *the Gospel of the resurrection* 10	*Tone* 5, *the Gospel of the resurrection* 3
Tone 2, *the Gospel of the resurrection* 11	*Tone* 6, *the Gospel of the resurrection* 4
Tone 3, *the Gospel of the resurrection* 1	*Tone* 7, *the Gospel of the resurrection* 5
Tone 4, *the Gospel of the resurrection* 2	*Tone* 8, *the Gospel of the resurrection* 6

Column III of the matutinal Gospels beginneth after the Elevation of the venerated cross.

Tone 1, *the Gospel of the resurrection* 7	*Tone* 5, *the Gospel of the resurrection* 11
Tone 2, *the Gospel of the resurrection* 8	*Tone* 6, *the Gospel of the resurrection* 1
Tone 3, *the Gospel of the resurrection* 9	*Tone* 7, *the Gospel of the resurrection* 2
Tone 4, *the Gospel of the resurrection* 10	*Tone* 8, *the Gospel of the resurrection* 3

Column IV of the matutinal Gospels beginneth with the Lent of the Nativity of Christ.

Tone 1, *the Gospel of the resurrection* 4	*Tone* 5, *the Gospel of the resurrection* 8
Tone 2, *the Gospel of the resurrection* 5	*Tone* 6, *the Gospel of the resurrection* 9
Tone 3, *the Gospel of the resurrection* 6	*Tone* 7, *the Gospel of the resurrection* 10
Tone 4, *the Gospel of the resurrection* 7	*Tone* 8, *the Gospel of the resurrection* 11

Column V of the matutinal Gospels beginneth after the Lord's Epiphany.

Tone 1, *the Gospel of the resurrection* 1	*Tone* 5, *the Gospel of the resurrection* 5
Tone 2, *the Gospel of the resurrection* 2	*Tone* 6, *the Gospel of the resurrection* 6
Tone 3, *the Gospel of the resurrection* 3	*Tone* 7, *the Gospel of the resurrection* 7
Tone 4, *the Gospel of the resurrection* 4	*Tone* 8, *the Gospel of the resurrection* 8

Column VI of the matutinal Gospels commenceth with the Holy Great Lent.

Tone 1, *the Gospel of the resurrection* 9	*Tone* 5, *the Gospel of the resurrection* 2
Tone 2, *the Gospel of the resurrection* 10	*Tone* 6, *the Gospel of the resurrection* 3
Tone 3, *the Gospel of the resurrection* 11	*Tone* 7, *the Gospel of the resurrection* 4
Tone 4, *the Gospel of the resurrection* 1	*Tone* 8, *the Gospel of the resurrection* 5

THE EXAPOSTEILARIA AND HEOTHINA.

The beginning of the Exaposteilaria and of the matutinal idiomelic, viz., evangelical, Sticheras (Heothina). These latter are the work of Emperor Leo the Wise, and the Exaposteilaria are the product of his son, Emperor Constantine.

The Exaposteilarion 1:

With the disciples let us go up into the mountain of Galilee to behold in faith Christ, declaring that He had obtained authority over all things both above and below; let us learn how He teacheth to baptize all nations in the name of the Father, and of the Son, and of the Holy Ghost, and that He abideth with the initiated, as He hath promised, unto the end of the world. [*The Theotokion:*

With the disciples didst Thou rejoice, O Theotokos-Virgin, that thou hast seen Christ risen from the grave on the third day, as He said; He did indeed appear unto them teaching and manifesting better things, and bidding them to baptize into the Father and Son, and Spirit, that we may believe His awaking and glorify thee, O Maiden.

The matutinal Stichera, Tone 1:

Whilst the disciples were coming up into the mountain at the ascension from the earth, the Lord stood before them; and having, after worshipping Him, been taught with regard to the power given them everywhere, they were sent into the universe to preach about the resurrection from the dead and the ascension into the heavens; unto them also hath promised to abide with them for ever the Truthful One, Christ the God and Saviour of our souls.

The Exaposteilarion 2:

Seeing the stone rolled away the myrrh-bearing women rejoiced, for they saw a youth sitting in the grave, and he said unto them: Behold, Christ is risen; tell Peter with the disciples;

hasten to the mountain of Galilee, there He will appear unto you, as He had said before to His friends. [*The Theotokion:* Just as an angel hath brought unto the Virgin the "Hail" before Thy conception, O Christ, so an angel also rolled away the stone from Thy grave; for the one, in the place of sorrow, was proclaiming symbols of unutterable joy, and the other, instead of death, was magnifying Thee as Giver of Life, and saying unto the women and the initiated about the resurrection.

The matutinal Stichera, Tone 2:

Unto the women that carrying myrrh came with Mary and were perplexed as to how they might attain their desire, there appeared the stone rolled away and a divine youth calming the tumult of their souls, for he said: Risen is the Lord Jesus; wherefore declare unto His heralds—the disciples—that they should run into Galilee to see Him risen from the dead, as Life-giver and Lord.

The Exaposteilarion, 3:

That Christ is risen, none may doubt; for He hath appeared unto Mary, then He was seen of those two that were going into the country, and then again He did appear unto the initiated eleven as they sat at meat; having sent these to baptize, He ascended into the heavens, whence He also came down, confirming the preaching by the multitude of signs. [*The Theotokion:* Do Thou, O Sun, that hast arisen to-day from the grave as a Bridegroom from a bridal-chamber, and that hast spoiled the hades and abolished death, send down upon us light through the intercessions of her who bare Thee,—a light that illumineth hearts and souls,—a light that instructeth all to walk in the paths of Thine ordinances and in the ways of peace.

The matutinal Stichera, Tone 3:

Disbelieving Mary Magdalene, when she announced the resurrection from the dead and the apparition of the Saviour, the disciples were reproached for the hardness of their hearts; but, having been armed with signs and wonders, they were sent forth to preach; and whilst Thou, O Lord, hast ascended unto the Origin of light, Thy Father, they have preached everywhere confirming the word by wonders; wherefore we, who have been enlightened by them, glorify Thy resurrection from the dead, O Lord, Lover of man.

The Exaposteilarion 4.

With radiant virtues let us see in the life-bearing tomb a man standing in shining garments, whereat the myrrh-bearing women had their faces bowed to the ground; let us be taught the awaking of the Heavenly Master and let us with Peter run unto the tomb of the Life and, marvelling at the work, continue to behold Christ. [*The Theotokion:*

Having said: Rejoice, Thou, O Lord, hast changed the sorrow of the forefathers, bringing into the world the joy of Thine awaking; wherefore, O Life-giver, send down through her who bare Thee the light thereof that enlighteneth the hearts, the light of Thy compassions that we may cry aloud unto Thee: O Lover of man, O God-man, glory to Thine awaking.

The matutinal Stichera. Tone 4.

It was very early in the morning, and the women have already come unto Thy tomb, O Christ, but the body which they were longing for was not found; being perplexed thereat they were thus addressed by those who in shining garments stood before them: Why seek ye the Living One among the dead? He is risen, as He hath foretold; why do ye not recall His words? Believing these, they announced what they saw, but their good-tidings were thought false, so sluggish still were the disciples; but Peter ran and, having seen, glorified within himself Thy wonders.

The Exaposteilarion 5:

The Life and the Way—Christ, risen from the dead, did walk together with Cleopas and Luke, and was also recognized of them in Emmaus in the breaking of bread; their souls and hearts were burning within them while He talked to them on the way, and by scriptures explained what He hath suffered; with them let us cry: He is risen and hath appeared unto Peter also. [*The Theotokion:*

I hymn Thy measureless mercy, O my Maker, since Thou hast emptied Thyself in order to put on and save the spoiled human nature, and, being God, wast pleased to become of the pure God's Maiden One like unto me and to descend even unto the hades, desiring, O Master, All-Compassionate, that I may be saved through the intercessions of her that bare Thee.

The matutinal Stichera. Tone 5.

Oh, the wisdom of Thy decrees, O Christ! How hast Thou enabled Peter, by Thy funeral shrouds alone, to come to the acknowledgment of Thine awaking; how joining Cleopas and Luke on their way Thou hast talked unto them, and in Thy converse didst not directly manifest Thyself; wherefore wast Thou also upbraided for being only a stranger in Jerusalem and for not having participated in the accomplishment of her counsels; but, ordering everything for the benefit of the new work, Thou hast expounded all the prophecies concerning Thee, and at the time of the blessing of bread becamest known unto them, whose hearts even before that were burning within them, and who, when the disciples were assembled, have with great clearness also proclaimed Thy resurrection; through which have mercy upon us.

The Exaposteilarion 6:

To shew forth that Thou, O Saviour, art a man according to substance, Thou standing in the midst (of disciples), after Thy resurrection from the dead, hast partaken of food and taught the baptism of penitence; and thereupon hast ascended unto Thy Heavenly Father, and to the disciples promised to send down the Paraclete, O Hyperdivine God-man, glory to Thine awaking. [*The Theotokion:*

The Maker of the creation and God of all hath taken human flesh of thy spotless blood, O all-holy Virgin, and all my corrupted nature hath made entirely new, having left it again after the child-birth, just as before child-birth; wherefore we all in faith praise thee, calling out: Hail, O Sovereign-Lady of the world.

The matutinal Stichera, Tone 6.

When Thou, O Christ—the true peace of God unto men—hast given Thy peace, after the awaking, unto the disciples, Thou hast proved them afraid, thinking they were seeing a spirit, but Thou hast set at rest the agitation of their souls, having shewn them Thy hands and feet; howbeit, whilst they were still doubting, Thou hast, by partaking of food and bringing unto their remembrance Thy teaching, opened their minds to understand the scriptures; after having given them also the promise of the Father and blessed them, Thou didst pass into heaven. Wherefore with them we worship Thee; O Lord glory to Thee.

The Exaposteilarion 7:

Because of the saying of Mary—they have taken away the Lord, Simon Peter and another initiated one of Christ, whom He loved, ran to the grave and, hurrying both, they found the linen clothes lying within alone and the napkin of the head was by itself; wherefore they were again silent until they saw Christ. [*The Theotokion:*

Great and most marvellous things hast Thou done for my sake, O my Christ greatly merciful; for from a Virgin Maiden wast Thou unspeakably born and didst accept the cross and, having endured death, Thou didst arise in glory and free our nature from death. Glory, O Christ, to Thy glory, glory to Thy power.

The matutinal Stichera. Tone 7.

Behold, darkness and early morn, and why, O Mary, dost thou stand at the tomb with yet a greater darkness in thy mind, asking: where and wherein had Jesus been placed? But see how the two disciples running together discovered the resurrection, through the linen clothes and the napkin, and remembered the scriptures thereon. With them and through them believing we hymn Thee, the Life-giving Christ.

The Exaposteilarion 8:

Seeing two angels inside the tomb, Mary was amazed and not knowing Christ asked Him as the Gardener: Sir, where hast thou laid the body of my Jesus; but having recognized in Him the Saviour Himself through being called of Him by the name, heard: Touch me not, I go away to the Father, tell unto My brethren. [*The Theotokion:*

O Maiden, thou hast ineffably given birth to One of the Trinity, Who is of two natures, of two energies, but of one hypostasis. Him then for ever entreat for those who in faith adore thee, that they may be delivered from every attack of the enemy, since we all have now recourse unto thee, O Sovereign-Lady Theotokos.

The matutinal Stichera. Tone 8.

The tears of S. Mary are not in vain being poured out warmly, for—behold—she was made worthy both of the teaching of angels and of the sight of Jesus Himself; but she still thinketh of earthly things as a weak woman, and is therefore sent away that she may not touch Thee, O Christ; and nevertheless she is sent as herald unto Thy disciples to whom she brought the good tidings, announcing Thine ascending to the paternal inheritance; with her make us also worthy of Thy manifestation, O Master Lord.

The Exaposteilarion 9.

Whilst the doors were closed, Thou, O Master, hast, on Thine entering, filled the apostles with the All-holy Spirit, having peacefully breathed on them; unto them also Thou hast said to bind and loose the sins, and eight days later hast shewn to Thomas Thy side and hands; with whom we also cry aloud: Lord and God Thou art. [*The Theotokion:*

As soon as thou didst behold thy Son risen from the grave on the third day, thou hast, O God's Bride, all-holy Virgin, laid aside all affliction with which as Mother thou wast stricken, when thou lookedst upon His sufferings, and together with His disciples, being filled with joy and honouring Him, dost thou hymn Him. Wherefore save those who now proclaim thee as Theotokos.

The matutinal Stichera. Tone 5.

When it was the end of times, Thou stoodest late on a Sabbath before the friends, O Christ, and by a miracle confirmedst miracle—Thy resurrection from the dead by entering through closed doors. But Thou hast filled the disciples with joy and given them the Holy Spirit together with authority of remitting sins; Thomas also hast Thou not left to become submerged through the tempest of unbelief. Wherefore grant unto us also knowledge of the truth and forgiveness of transgressions, O Compassionate Lord.

The Exaposteilarion, 10:

The sea of Tiberias had once a fishing: Nathaniel with Peter, the children of Zebedee with two others and Thomas; these, having at the bidding of Christ cast their net on the right hand side, dragged out a multitude of fishes; Whom recognizing Peter waded towards Him; unto them thus appearing the third time, He shewed them both bread and fish upon coals [*The Theotokion:* The Lord risen from the grave on the third day do, O Virgin, entreat for those who hymn and lovingly bless thee; since in thee we all have a refuge of salvation and a mediatrix with Him, for we are the heritage and servants, O Theotokos, and unto thy protection we all look up.

The matutinal Stichera, Tone 6:

After the descent into the hades and the resurrection from the dead, the disciples sorrowing, as it behoved, on account of the separation from Thee, O Christ, have returned to their work; once more they handled ships and nets, but nowhere a catch; howbeit Thou, O Saviour, appearing unto them as Master of everything, biddest them to cast the nets upon the right hand side, and the word was soon become a deed—there was a great multitude of fishes and upon the land a hospitable supper ready;

the disciples having then partaken thereof, do Thou, O Lord —Lover of man, make now also us worthy to intellectually enjoy it.

The Exaposteilarion IV:

After the divine awaking, having thrice asked: Lovest thou Me, the Lord proposeth Peter as chief pastor of His own sheep; who seeing him whom Jesus loved following after, enquired of the Master: But what of this one? If I will, He rejoined, that he tarry till I come again also, what is that to thee, friend Peter. [*The Theotokion:*

O fearful mystery! O most marvellous wonder! death was utterly destroyed by death! Who then will not hymn thee? and who will not worship Thy resurrection, O Word, and her who without corruption gave birth to Thee in flesh, the Theotokos? Through her intercessions do thou deliver all from gehenna.

The matutinal Stichera, Tone 8:

Manifesting Thyself unto Thy disciples, O Saviour, after the resurrection, to Simon hast thou given the pasturage of the sheep, demanding in requital for love the care of the flock; wherefore hast Thou said: If thou lovest Me, Peter, feed My lambs, feed My sheep. And he, shewing straightway his tenderness, enquired about the other disciple. Through their intercessions, O Christ, preserve Thy flock from wolves that ruin it.

THE GOSPELS OF THE RESURRECTION.

The First Gospel of the resurrection, from St. Matthew, Section 116 (28, 16-20).

At that time the eleven disciples went away into Galilee, into a mountain where Jesus had appointed them. And when they saw Him, they worshipped Him: but some doubted. And Jesus came and spake unto them, saying: all power is given unto Me in heaven and in earth. Go ye therefore, and teach all nations, baptizing them in the name of the Father, and of the Son, and of the Holy Ghost; teaching them to observe all things whatsoever I have commanded you: and, lo, I am with you alway, even unto the end of the world. Amen.

The Second Gospel of the resurrection, from St. Mark, Section 70 (16, 1-8).

At that time when the Sabbath was passed, Mary Magdalene, and Mary the mother of James, and Salome, had bought sweet spices, that they might come and anoint Him. And very early in the morning the first day of the week, they came unto the sepulchre at the rising of the sun. And they said among themselves: Who shall roll us away the stone from the door of the sepulchre? And when they looked, they saw that the stone was rolled away; for it was very great. And entering into the sepulchre, they saw a young man sitting on the right side, clothed in a long white garment; and they were affrighted. And He saith unto them: Be not affrighted! Ye seek Jesus of Nazareth, Which was crucified? He is risen; He is not here: behold the place where they laid Him. But go your way, tell His disciples and Peter that He goeth before you into Galilee: there shall ye see Him, as He said unto you. And they went out quickly, and fled from the sepulchre; for they trembled and were amazed: neither said they any thing to any man; for they were afraid. Amen.

The Third Gospel of the resurrection, from St. Mark, Section 71 (16, 9-20).

At that time when Jesus was risen early the first day of the week, He appeared first to Mary Magdalene, out of whom He had cast seven devils. And she went and told them that had been with Him, as they mourned and wept. And they, when they had heard that He was alive, and had been seen of her, believed not. After that He appeared in another form unto two of them, as they walked, and went into the country. And they went and told it unto the residue: neither believed they them. Lastly He appeared unto the eleven as they sat at meat, and upbraided them with their unbelief and hardness of heart, because they believed not them which had seen Him after He was risen. And He said unto them: Go ye into all the world, and preach the gospel to every creature. He that believeth and is baptized shall be saved; but he that believeth not shall be condemned. And these signs shall follow them that believe: In My name shall they cast out devils; they shall speak with new tongues; they shall take up serpents; and if they drink any deadly thing, it shall not hurt them; they shall lay hands on the sick, and they shall recover. So then after the Lord had spoken unto them, He ascended up into heaven, and sat on the right hand of God. And they went forth and preached everywhere, the Lord working with them, and confirming the word with signs following. Amen.

The Fourth Gospel of the resurrection, from St. Luke, Section 112 (24, 1-12).

At that time upon the first day of the week, very early in the morning, the women came unto the sepulchre, bringing the spices which they had prepared, and certain others with them. And they found the stone rolled away from the sepulchre. And they entered in, and found not the body of the Lord Jesus. And it came to pass as they were much perplexed thereabout, behold, two men stood by them in shining garments. And as they were afraid, and bowed down their faces to the earth, they said unto them: Why seek ye the Living among the dead? He is not here, but is risen: remember how He spake unto you when He was yet in Galilee, saying: the Son of man must be delivered into the hands of sinful men, and be crucified, and the third day rise again. And they remembered His words, and returned from the sepulchre, and told all these things unto the eleven, and to all the rest. It was Mary Magdalene, and Joanna, and Mary the mother of James, and other women that were with them, which told these things unto the apostles. And their words seemed to them as idle tales, and they believed them not. Then arose Peter, and ran unto the sepulchre; and stooping down, he beheld the linen clothes laid by themselves, and departed, wondering in himself at that which was come to pass. Amen.

The Fifth Gospel of the resurrection, from St. Luke, Section 113 (24, 13-35).

At that time Peter arose and ran unto the sepulchre; and stooping down, he beheld the linen clothes laid by themselves, and departed, wondering in himself at that which was come to pass. And, behold, two of them went that same day to a village called Emmaus, which was from Jerusalem about threescore furlongs. And they talked together of all these things which had happened. And it came to pass, that, while they communed together and reasoned, Jesus Himself drew near, and went with them. But their eyes were holden that they should not know Him. And He said unto them: What manner of communications are these that ye have one to another, as ye walk, and are sad? And the one of them, whose name was Cleopas, answering said unto Him: Art thou only a stranger in Jerusalem, and hast not known the things which are come to pass there in these days? And He said unto them: What things? And they said unto Him: Concerning Jesus of Nazareth, Which was a prophet mighty in deed and word before God and all the people; and how the chief priests and our rulers delivered Him to be condemned to death, and have crucified Him. But we trusted that it had been He Which should have redeemed Israel: and beside all this, to day is the third day since these things were done. Yea, and certain women also of our company made us astonished, which were early at the sepulchre; and when they found not his body, they came, saying, that they had also seen a vision of angels, which said that he was alive. And certain of them which were with us went to the sepulchre, and found it even so as the women had said: but Him they saw not Then He said unto them: O fools, and slow of heart to believe all that the prophets have spoken: Ought not Christ to have suffered these things, and to enter into His glory? And beginning at Moses and all the prophets, He expounded unto them in all the scriptures the things concerning Himself. And they drew nigh unto the village, whither they went; and he made as though He would have gone further. But they constrained Him, saying: Abide with us; for it is toward evening, and the day is far spent. And He went in to tarry with them. And it came to pass, as He sat at meat with them, He took bread and blessed it, and brake, and gave to them. And their eyes were opened, and they knew Him; and He vanished out of their sight. And they said one to another: Did not our heart burn within us, while He talked with us by the way, and while He opened to us the scriptures? And they rose up the same hour, and returned to Jerusalem, and found the eleven gathered together, and them that were with them, saying: the Lord is risen indeed, and hath appeared to Simon. And they told what things were done in the way, and how He was known of them in breaking of bread. Amen.

The Sixth Gospel of the resurrection, from St. Luke, Section 114 (24, 36-53):

At that time Jesus rose from the dead, stood in the midst of His disciples, and said unto them: Peace be unto you. But they were terrified and affrighted, and supposed that they had seen a spirit. And He said unto them: Why are ye troubled? and why do thoughts arise in your hearts? Behold My hands and My feet, that it is I Myself: handle Me, and see; for a spirit hath not flesh and bones, as ye see Me have. And when

He had thus spoken, He showed them His hands and His feet. And while they yet believed not for joy, and wondered, He said unto them: Have ye here any meat? And they gave Him a piece of a broiled fish, and of an honeycomb. And He took it, and did eat before them. And He said unto them: These are the words which I spake unto you, while I was yet with you, that all things must be fulfilled, which were written in the law of Moses, and in the prophets, and in the psalms, concerning Me. Then opened He their understanding, that they might understand the scriptures, and said unto them: Thus it is written, and thus it behoved Christ to suffer, and to rise from the dead the third day; and that repentance and remission of sins should be preached in His name among all nations, beginning at Jerusalem. And ye are witnesses of these things. And, behold, I send the promise of my Father upon you: but tarry ye in the city of Jerusalem, until ye be endued with power from on high. And He led them out as far as to Bethany, and He lifted up His hands, and blessed them. And it came to pass, while He blessed them, He was parted from them, and carried up into heaven. And they worshipped Him, and returned to Jerusalem with great joy; and were continually in the temple, praising and blessing God. Amen.

The Seventh Gospel of the resurrection, from St. John, Section 63 (20, 1-10).

At that time, on the first day of the week, Mary Magdalene came early, when it was yet dark, unto the sepulchre, and seeth the stone taken away from the sepulchre. Then she ran, and came to Simon Peter, and to the other disciple, whom Jesus loved, and said unto them: They have taken away the Lord out of the sepulchre, and I know not where they have laid Him. Peter therefore went forth, and that other disciple, and came to the sepulchre. And they ran both together; and the other disciple did outrun Peter, and came first to the sepulchre. And stooping down, and looking in, he saw the linen clothes lying; yet entered he not in. Then came Simon Peter following him, and went into the sepulchre, and saw the linen clothes lie, and the napkin that was about His head, not lying with the linen clothes, but wrapped together in a place by itself. Then entered in also that other disciple, which came first to the sepulchre, and he saw, and believed. For as yet they knew not the scripture, that He must rise again from the dead. Then the disciples went away again unto their own home. Amen.

The Eighth Gospel of the resurrection, from St. John, Section 64, (20, 11-18).

At that time Mary stood without at the sepulchre weeping; and as she wept, she stooped down into the sepulchre, and saw two angels in white sitting, the one at the head, and the other at the feet, where the body of Jesus had lain. And they said unto her: Woman, why weepest thou? She said unto them: Because they have taken away my Lord, and I know not where they have laid Him. And when she had thus said, she turned herself back, and saw Jesus standing, and knew not that it was Jesus. Jesus said unto her: Woman, why weepest thou? whom seekest thou? She, supposing Him to be the gardener, said unto Him: Sir, if thou have taken Him hence, tell me where thou hast laid Him, and I will take Him away. Jesus said unto her: Mary! She turned herself, and said unto Him: Rabboni; which is to say, Master. Jesus said unto her: Touch Me not; for I am not yet ascended to My Father: but go to My brethren, and say unto them, I ascend unto My Father, and your Father; and to My God, and your God. Mary Magdalene came and told the disciples that she had seen the Lord, and that He had spoken these things unto her. Amen.

The Ninth Gospel of the resurrection, from St. John, Section 65 (20, 19-31).

At that time the same day at evening, being the first day of the week, when the doors were shut where the disciples were assembled for fear of the Jews, came Jesus and stood in the midst, and said unto them: Peace be unto you. And when He had so said, He shewed unto them His hands and His side. Then were the disciples glad, when they saw the Lord. Then said Jesus to them again: Peace be unto you: as My Father hath sent Me, even so send I you. And when He had said this, He breathed on them, and saith unto them: Receive ye the Holy Ghost; whose soever sins ye remit, they are remitted unto them; and whose soever sins ye retain, they are retained. But Thomas, one of the twelve, called Didymus, was not with them when Jesus came. The other disciples therefore said unto him: We have seen the Lord. But he said unto them: Except I shall see in His hands the print of the nails, and put my finger into the print of the nails, and thrust my hand into His side, I will not believe. And after eight days again His disciples were within, and Thomas with them; then came Jesus, the doors being shut, and stood in the midst, and said: Peace be unto you. Then said He to Thomas: Reach hither thy finger, and behold My hands; and reach hither thy hand, and thrust it into My side; and be not faithless, but believing. And Thomas answered and said unto Him: My Lord and my God. Jesus said unto him: Thomas, because thou hast seen Me, thou hast believed; blessed are they that have not seen, and yet have believed. And many other signs truly did Jesus in the presence of His disciples, which are not written in this book; but these are written, that ye might believe that Jesus is the Christ, the Son of God; and that believing ye may have life in His name. Amen.

The Tenth Gospel of the resurrection, from St. John, Section 66 (21, 1-14).

At that time Jesus shewed Himself to the disciples at the sea of Tiberias; and on this wise shewed He Himself. There were together Simon Peter, and Thomas called Didymus, and Nathanael of Cana in Galilee, and the sons of Zebedee, and two other of His disciples. Simon Peter said unto them: I go a fishing. They said unto Him: We also go with thee. They went forth, and entered into a ship immediately; and that night they caught nothing. But when the morning was now come, Jesus stood on the shore: but the disciples knew not that it was

Jesus. Then Jesus said unto them: Children, have ye any meat? They answered Him: No. And He said unto them: Cast the net on the right side of the ship, and ye shall find. They cast therefore, and now they were not able to draw it for the multitude of fishes. Therefore that disciple whom Jesus loved said unto Peter: It is the Lord. Now when Simon Peter heard that it was the Lord, he girt his fisher's coat unto him (for he was naked), and did cast himself into the sea. And the other disciples came in a little ship; (for they were not far from land, but as it were 200 cubits), dragging the net with fishes. As soon then as they were come to land, they saw a fire of coals there, and fish laid thereon, and bread. Jesus said unto them: Bring of the fish which ye have now caught. Simon Peter went up, and drew the net to land full of great fishes, an hundred and fifty and three: and for all there were so many, yet was not the net broken. Jesus said unto them: Come and dine. And none of the disciples durst ask Him: Who art Thou? knowing that it was the Lord. Jesus then came, and took bread, and gave them, and fish likewise. This is now the third time that Jesus shewed Himself to His disciples, after that He was risen from the dead. Amen.

The Eleventh Gospel of the resurrection, from St. John, Section 67 (21, 15-25).

At that time Jesus shewed Himself to His disciples after that He was risen from the dead and said to Simon Peter: Simon, son of Jonas, lovest thou Me more than these? He said unto Him: Yea, Lord; Thou knowest that I love Thee. He said unto him: Feed My lambs. He said to him again the second time: Simon, son of Jonas, lovest thou Me? He said unto Him: Yea, Lord; Thou knowest that I love Thee. He said unto him: Feed My sheep. He said unto him the third time: Simon, son of Jonas, lovest thou Me? Peter was grieved because He said unto him the third time: Lovest thou Me? And he said unto Him: Lord, Thou knowest all things; Thou knowest that I love Thee. Jesus said unto him: Feed My sheep. Verily, verily, I say unto thee: When thou wast young, thou girdest thyself, and walkedst whither thou wouldest: but when thou shalt be old, thou shalt stretch forth thy hands, and another shall gird thee, and lead thee whither thou wouldest not. This spake He, signifying by what death he should glorify God. And when He had spoken this, He said unto him: Follow Me. Then Peter, turning about, seeth the disciple whom Jesus loved following; which also leaned on His breast at supper, and said: Lord, which is he that betrayeth Thee? Peter seeing him said to Jesus: Lord, and what of this one? Jesus said unto him: If I will that he tarry till I come, what is that to thee? follow thou Me. Then went this saying abroad among the brethren, that that disciple should not die; yet Jesus said not unto him He shall not die; but, if I will that he tarry till I come, what is that to thee? This is the disciple which testifieth of these things, and wrote these things; and I know that his testimony is true. And there are also many other things which Jesus did, the which, if they should be written every one, I suppose that even the world itself could not contain the books that should be written. Amen.

SERVICE FOR THOSE FALLEN ASLEEP.

On Friday evening at the conclusion of the Great Vespers the Priest saith : Blessed is our God..., censing the coliba crosswise. We say : The Trisagion. And at the end of Our Father, the Priest maketh the Exclamation : For Thine is the Kingdom... Thereupon, Lord, have mercy, 12 *times...Glory...Both now...... Come, let us adore...thrice.*

Psalm 90.

He that dwelleth under the wardship of the Most High under the shelter of the God of heavens shall abide. He will say to the Lord: Thou art my protector and my refuge, my God, and in Him shall I trust. For He shall deliver thee from the snare of the fowlers and from the noise of uproar; He shall shadow thee with His pinions and under the cover of His wings thou shalt feel confident; as armour shall His truth encircle thee. Thou shalt not be afraid for a terror by night, nor for an arrow that flieth by day, for anything that walketh in darkness, nor for an encounter and a midday demon. A thousand shall fall at thy side and ten thousand at thy right hand, but it shall not come nigh thee: only with thine eyes shalt thou behold and see the reward of the wicked. For with " Lord, Thou art my trust," hast thou made the Most High thy refuge. There shall no evil befall thee, neither shall any calamity come nigh thy body (*tent*); for He shall command His angels concerning thee—to keep thee in all thy ways. They shall take thee up in their hands, lest thou dash thy foot against a stone; thou shalt tread upon the adder and the basilisk; the lion and the serpent shalt thou trample under foot. Because he hath trusted in Me, will I also therefore deliver him; I shall shelter him, for he hath acknowledged My name. He shall call upon Me, and I will hearken unto him:

with him am I in trouble, I will deliver him, and glorify him; with long life will I satisfy him and shew him my salvation.

Glory ... Both now ... Alleluia thrice.

And there is said the Ectene for the departed:

In peace let us pray to the Lord. *The Choir*: Lord have mercy.

For the peace from above and the salvation of our souls, let us pray to the Lord.

For the remission of sins of those of blessed memory who have departed this life, let us pray to the Lord.

For the ever-remembered servants of God (*mentioned by name*), that they may obtain rest, tranquillity and blessed remembrance, let us pray to the Lord.

That He may forgive them every transgression both voluntary and involuntary, let us pray to the Lord.

That they may appear uncondemned before the dreadful throne of the Lord of glory, let us pray to the Lord.

For them that weep and grieve, looking for the consolation of Christ, let us pray to the Lord.

That He may set them free from every ailment and from sorrow and sighing, and cause them to dwell wherein shineth the light of God's countenance,—let us pray to the Lord.

That the Lord our God may settle their souls in a place of light, a place of refreshment, a place of repose where all the just do dwell,—let us pray to the Lord.

That they may be numbered amongst those that are in the bosom of Abraham, of Isaac, and of Jacob, let us pray to the Lord.

That we may be delivered from all tribulation, wrath and necessity, let us pray to the Lord.

Succour and save us, have mercy and preserve us, O God, by Thy mercy.

Having prayed for God's mercy, and the Kingdom of heaven, and for the remission of sins, both unto them and unto ourselves, let us commend one another and all our life unto Christ our God. *And we say:* To Thee, O Lord.

The Priest saith the Exclamation : For Thou art the resurrection and the life, and the repose of Thy servants, that are fallen asleep, the ever-remembered founders, our fathers and brethren, all the orthodox Christians lying here and everywhere, O Christ our God; and unto Thee do we send up glory together with Thine Unoriginate Father, and Thine All-holy, and Good, and Life-giving Spirit, both now and ever, and unto the ages of ages... Amen.

Thereupon, Alleluia, thrice, Tone 8. *We say these Verses* :

Verse 1 : Blessed art those whom Thou hast chosen and received unto Thee, O Lord (Psalm 64, 5).

Verse 2 : Their remembrance is from generation to generation (Psalm 101, 13).

Verse 3 : Their souls shall dwell at ease (Psalm 24, 13).

Thereupon, the Troparion, Tone 8 :

Thou Who in the depth of wisdom and with love to man makest everything and givest to every one all that is beneficial, the sole Author of all, grant, O Lord, repose to the souls of Thy servants; for they did put their trust in Thee, our Creator and Maker and God.

Twice. Glory...Both now...the Theotokion :

In thee we have a wall and a haven and an intercessor acceptable to God Whom thou didst bear, O Theotokos unmarried, who art the salvation of the faithful.

Thereupon, the Cathisma : Blessed are the blameless...

Refrain : Remember, O Lord, the souls of Thy servants.

We sing it in Tone 2. *Then another Choir taketh up the second Verse, and in successive order all the other Verses are sung by both the Choirs. And we divide the Cathisma into two parts, do not say, however, at the end of the first part : Glory...Both now..., but at once the following Verse :*

For if my delight had not been in Thy law, then I should have perished in my trouble. I will never forget Thy commandments, for with them Thou hast quickened me. *Thrice.*

And the Priest saith the Ectene for the departed:

Again and again let us pray to the Lord.

The Choir: Lord, have mercy.

Again we pray for the repose of the souls of the servants of God who have fallen asleep (*mentioned by name*) and that they may be forgiven every transgression both voluntary and involuntary. *The Choir:* Lord, have mercy.

That the Lord God may settle their souls, where the righteous repose. *The Choir:* Lord, have mercy.

The mercy of God, the Kingdom of heaven and the remission of their sins—let us ask of Christ, our Immortal King and God. *The Choir:* Lord, have mercy.

The Deacon: Let us pray to the Lord. *The Choir:* Lord, have mercy (*forty*).

The Priest saith secretly the following prayer:

O God of spirits and of all flesh, Who hast trampled upon death and brought to naught the devil, and hast bestowed life upon this world of Thine, do Thou Thyself, O Lord, give rest to the souls of Thy servants that have fallen asleep (*mentioned by name*) in a place of light, a place of refreshment, a place of repose whence pain and sorrow and sighing have fled away. Every sin committed by them in word, or deed, or thought, do Thou, as a Good God and Lover of men, forgive; for there is no man that liveth and sinneth not; for Thou alone art without sin, Thy righteousness is righteousness for ever, and Thy word is truth. *The Exclamation:* For thou art the resurrection, life and the repose......*Refrain:* Give rest, O Lord, unto the souls of Thy servants. *And alternately are said the remaining Verses by both the Choirs. At the end we sing the Verse:* O let my soul live and it shall praise Thee...(*thrice*) *to the end.*

Thereupon are sung the Troparia of the departed, Tone 5.

Refrain: Blessed art Thou, O Lord; teach me Thy justifications.

The choir of the saints have found the fountain of life and the door of paradise; O that I also may discover the way through penitence! I am the lost sheep, call me back, O Saviour, and save me.

Refrain: Blessed art Thou, O Lord, teach me Thy justifications.

Ye that have preached the Lamb of God and yourselves having been immolated as lambs, were, O holy ones, translated into a life that never groweth old nor perisheth, do assiduously entreat Him, O martyrs, to grant us forgiveness of our debts.

Refrain: Blessed art Thou, O Lord, teach me Thy justifications.

Ye that went along the narrow path of tribulation, all ye that in your life time the cross as a yoke have taken up and followed Me in faith, come and enjoy the rewards and the heavenly crowns which I have prepared for you.

Refrain: Blessed art Thou, O Lord, teach me Thy justifications.

I am an image of Thine ineffable glory, though I also carry the stigmata of my failings; take compassion on Thy creature, O Lord, and cleanse me according to Thy commiseration, and grant unto me the desired fatherland, making me again a dweller of paradise.

Refrain: Blessed art Thou, O Lord, teach me Thy justifications.

Thou that of old createdest me out of nothing and with Thine own divine image hast honoured, but on account of the violation of Thy commandment didst return me again into the earth, out of which I was taken, do bring me up afresh unto the likeness that I may again be fashioned in the former beauty.

Refrain: Blessed art Thou, O Lord, teach me Thy justifications.

Lay at rest, O God, Thy servants and order them in paradise, wherein, O Lord, the choirs of the holy and righteous shine as stars; give rest unto Thy departed servants, disregarding all their sins.

Glory (*of the Trinity*) *:* Let us piously hymn the three-fold lustre of the One Godhead, crying out: Holy art Thou, the Unoriginate Father, the Co-Unoriginate Son and the Divine Spirit; enlighten us worshipping Thee in faith, and pluck us out of the eternal fire.

Both now (*the Theotokion*) *:* Hail thou, O pure one, that hast born in flesh God unto salvation of all, and through whom the human race hath found the salvation; may we attain paradise through thee, O Theotokos, pure and blessed.

Thereupon, Alleluia, thrice. Then, Ectene. And the Priest readeth the names of the departed in the same order as hath been before set forth, between the two divisions of "the Blameless." But if "the Blameless" be not sung, then after Alleluia we say the Troparion: Thou Who in the depth of wisdom...and the Theotokion thereof. And straightway: Blessed art Thou, O Lord...Thereupon the Troparia: The choir of the saints have found...And the rest.

Thereupon the Priest readeth the names of the departed, as set forth before.

And we say the Cathismaton for the departed, Tone 5 *:*

Give repose, O our Saviour, with the righteous unto Thy servants and order them in Thy Courts, as it is written, disregarding, as a Good One, their transgressions, both voluntary and involuntary, and everything they have committed either with knowledge or unknowingly, O Lover of man.

Glory...Both now...the Theotokion:

O Christ the God, that hast shone forth unto the world from the Virgin and through her hast manifested the sons of light have mercy upon us.

Thereupon, Psalm 50: Have mercy upon us, O God...

Thereupon, the Canon for the departed from the Octoechos of the Tone that happeneth to be, with 4 Troparia. After the 3rd Ode, the Heirmos and Ectene. And the Priest readeth the names of the departed as set forth before, between the two parts of "the Blameless."

The Exclamation: For Thou art the resurrection and the life...

Thereupon the Cathismaton, Tone 6:

Of a truth everything is vanity, and the life is but a shadow and a dream; for in vain doth every earth-born strenuously strive, as the scripture saith: when we obtain mastery over the world, we come to dwell within a grave where are gathered together both the kings and the needy. Wherefore, O Christ the God, do give rest unto the departed, as Lover of man.

Glory...Both now...the Theotokion:

O all-holy Theotokos, throughout the period of my life, abandon me not, unto human protection entrust me not, but do thyself defend me and have mercy on me.

After the 6*th Ode the Heirmos and Ectene. And the Priest readeth the names of the departed as is set forth before.*

The Exclamation: For Thou art the resurrection and the life...

Thereupon the Contakion, Tone 8:

With Thy saints, O Christ, give Thou rest to the souls of Thy servants wherein there is neither sickness nor sorrow and lamentation, but life unending.

The Oikos: Thou only art immortal that didst create and fashion man; but we of the earth were formed of earth and unto the same earth shall come, even as Thou didst ordain that didst fashion me and saidst unto me: Dust thou art and unto dust shalt thou return, whither we all men shall go, making as lamentation over the grave this song: Alleluia. *Thrice.*

After the 9*th Ode the Priest saith:* The Theotokos and Mother of the Light let us magnify in hymns. *The Choir:* The spirits and souls of the righteous shall praise Thee, O Lord.

[*And we sing the Heirmos of the* 9*th Ode:*

Thereupon, the Trisagion. And after "Our Father" we say these Troparia, Tone 4:

With the spirits of the righteous that have finished their course give rest, O Saviour, to the souls of Thy servants, keeping them in that blessed life which is with Thee, O Lover of man.

In Thy resting-place, O Lord, where all Thy saints repose give rest likewise to the soul of Thy servants, since Thou alone art the Lover of man. [*Glory ...*

Thou art the God Who didst descend into the hades and didst loose the chains of those that were bound; do Thou Thyself give rest likewise to the souls of Thy servants. [*Both now...*

O only chaste and undefiled Virgin who didst without seed conceive God, intercede that their souls may be saved.

Thereupon the Priest saith the Ectene:

Have mercy upon us, O God, according to Thy great mercy, we beseech Thee, hearken and have mercy.

[*The Choir: Lord have mercy, thrice:*

Again we beseech for the repose of the souls of the servants of God who have fallen asleep (*mentioned by name*) and that they may be forgiven every transgression both voluntary and involuntary. [*The Choir:* Lord, have mercy, *thrice:*

That the Lord God would order their souls where the righteous repose. [*The Choir:* Lord, have mercy, *thrice:*

The mercy of God, the Kingdom of the heavens and the remission of sins—let us ask of Christ, our Immortal King and God. [*The Choir:* Grant, O Lord.

The Deacon: Let us pray to the Lord.

The Priest: O God of spirits ...

And he readeth out the names of our long departed fathers and brethren—the orthodox christians both lying here and everywhere.

Thereupon the Exclamation: For Thou art the resurrection and the life ...

The Priest or Deacon saith: Wisdom! *And we:* More honourable than the cherubim.

The Priest: Glory to Thee, O Christ the God, our hope, glory to Thee. *And we:* Glory ...

Both now ...Lord, have mercy *thrice.* Give the blessing.

[*The Priest saith the Dismission:*

May Christ, our true God, Who arose from the dead, by the prayers of His most pure Mother, of the holy, glorious and all-laudable apostles, of our reverend and God-bearing fathers and of all saints, settle the souls of His servants departed from us in the tabernacles of the just, repose them in the bosom of Abraham and number with the righteous, and have mercy upon us, as Good One and Lover of man.

And after the Dismission the Deacon saith aloud as followeth :

In a blessed falling asleep grant, O Lord, everlasting rest unto Thy departed servants (*mentioned by name*) and cause them to be held in everlasting remembrance.

And the Choir sing : Everlasting remembrance. *Thrice.*

And where there is no Deacon, the Choir sing : Unto the servants of God (mentioned by name), fallen asleep, everlasting remembrance.

To the glory of the Holy, One-substanced, Life-giving and Indivisible Trinity of the Father, and of the Son and of the Holy Ghost, in the reign of the Right-faithful Autocrat, our Great Sovereign, Emperor Nicholas Alexandrovitch of all the Russias, in the time of his Consort, the Right-faithful Lady, Empress Alexanda Feodorovna, of his Mother, the Right faithful Lady, Empress Mary Feodorovna and of his Heir, the orthodox Lord, Cesarevitch and Grand Duke George Alexandrovitch ; in the time of the orthodox Lord, Grand Duke Michael Alexandrovitch ; in the time of the orthodox Lord, Grand Duke Vladimir Alexandrovitch, of his Consort the Grand Duchess Mary Pavlevna, and of the orthodox Lords, Grand Dukes : Cyril, Boris and Andrew Vladimirovitchi ; in the time of the orthodox Lord, Grand Duke Alexis Alexandrovitch, of the orthodox Lord, Grand Duke Serge Alexandrovitch and of his Consort the orthodox Lady, Grand Duchess Elisabeth Feodorovna ; in the time of the orthodox Lord, Grand Duke Paul Alexandrovitch and of the orthodox Lord, Grand Duke Demetrius Pavlovitch ; in the time of the orthodox Lady, Grand Duchess Alexandra Josephovna, of the orthodox Lord, Grand Duke Nicholas Constantinovitch, of the orthodox Lord, Grand Duke Constantine Constantinovitch, and of his Consort the Grand Duchess Elisabeth Mavrikievna, and of the orthodox Lord, Grand Duke Demetrius Constantinovitch ; in the time of the orthodox Lady, Grand Duchess Alexandra Petrovna, of the orthodox Lord, Grand Duke Nicholas Nicholaevitch, of the orthodox Lord, Grand Duke Peter Nicholaevitch, and of his Consort, the orthodox Lady, Grand Duchess Militza Nicholaevna; in the time of orthodox Lord, Grand Duke Michael Nicholaevitch, of the orthodox Lords, Grand Dukes : Nicholas, Michael, and George Michaelovitchi, of the orthodox Lord, Grand Duke Alexander Michaelovitch and of his Consort, the orthodox Lady, Grand Duchess Xenia Alexandrovna, and of the orthodox Lord, Grand Duke Serge Michaelovitch ; in the time of the orthodox Ladies, Grand Duchesses : Olga and Tatiana Nicholaevny, of the orthodox Lady, Grand Duchess Olga Alexandrovna, of the orthodox Lady, Grand Duchess Helena Vladimirovna, of the orthodox Lady, Grand Duchess Mary Pavlovna ; in the time of the orthodox Lady, Grand Duchess Mary Alexandrova and of her Consort ; in the time of the Queen of the Hellenes Olga Constantinovna and of her Consort, of the Grand Duchess Vera Constantinovna, of the Grand Duchess Anastasia Michaelovna ; and with the blessing of the Right Reverend Nicholas, Lord Bishop of Alaska and of the Aleutan Islands, this translation of "Octoechos, or the Book of Eight Tones, a Primer containing the Sunday service in Eight Tones" from the first edition of the Most Holy Governing Synod of Russia of 1891 hath been printed in the capital city of London, at the Dryden Press office, in its first impression in the year of the world 7407, and in the year from the incarnation of God the Word 1898, in the month of May, the sixty-first year of the reign of Queen Victoria, whom may God preserve.

CPSIA information can be obtained at www.ICGtesting.com
Printed in the USA
BVOW05s1111080315

390772BV00007B/150/P